ALEXANDER GRAHAM BELL AND THE TELEPHONE

MILESTONES

IN
AMERICAN HISTORY

MILESTONES
IN
AMERICAN HISTORY

ALEXANDER GRAHAM BELL AND THE TELEPHONE

THE INVENTION THAT CHANGED COMMUNICATION

SAMUEL WILLARD CROMPTON

CHELSEA HOUSE
PUBLISHERS
An imprint of Infobase Publishing

Alexander Graham Bell and the Telephone

Chelsea House
An imprint of Infobase Publishing
132 West 31st Street
New York, NY 10001

Library of Congress Cataloging-in-Publication Data

Crompton, Samuel Willard.
  Alexander Graham Bell and the telephone : the invention that changed communication / Samuel Willard Crompton.
    p. cm. — (Milestones in American history)
  Includes bibliographical references and index.
  ISBN 978-1-60413-004-1 (hardcover)
  1. Bell, Alexander Graham, 1847–1922—Juvenile literature. 2. Inventors—United States—Biography. 3. Telephone—History—Juvenile literature. I. Title. II. Series.
  TK6143.B4C76 2009
  621.385092—dc22
  [B]   2008025313

Chelsea House books are available at special discounts when purchased in bulk quantities for businesses, associations, institutions, or sales promotions. Please call our Special Sales Department in New York at (212) 967-8800 or (800) 322-8755.

You can find Chelsea House on the World Wide Web at http://www.chelseahouse.com

Text design by Erik Lindstrom
Cover design by Ben Peterson
Composition by North Market Street Graphics
Cover printed by Yurchak Printing, Landisville, Pa.
Book printed and bound by Yurchak Printing, Landisville, Pa.

Printed in the United States of America

All links and Web addresses were checked and verified to be correct at the time of publication. Because of the dynamic nature of the Web, some addresses and links may have changed since publication and may no longer be valid.

CONTENTS

School's Out

The last day of school at the Boston School for Deaf Mutes (now called the Horace Mann School for the Deaf and Hard of Hearing) was June 21, 1871. The children, who were eager to be finished for the year, had been working on their ability to read lips, both visually and with the help of their hands, for the last nine months. Their parents had entrusted them to this school at a time when there were relatively few places that taught deaf children. Before the start of their summer vacation, however, the children had to pose for a portrait with the school's faculty.

Looking at the photograph today, we can see the important school officials. Standing on the top level of the stairway, on the left-hand side, is a white-haired, distinguished-looking man. This is Reverend Dexter King, the founder of the school. In looks and attitude, he was like the famous Yankee writer

Ralph Waldo Emerson, a man of great talent and serene temperament.

On the fourth stair down from the top, and one in from the left-hand side, sits Sarah Fuller, the principal of the school. Describing her, a colleague said, "I never saw *Love, Goodness* and *Firmness* so blended in one face before ... Her abilities seem very great but she is very modest about them, and she is *overflowing* with genuine goodness *towards* the children."[1]

Seated on that same set of stairs, two persons to Sarah Fuller's right, is Mary True. Less well-known than Dexter King or Sarah Fuller, True came from Maine and her lifetime occupation was to teach the deaf. For several years, her principal charge was student Mabel Gardiner Hubbard, away on a trip to Germany with her family when the photo was taken.

Many faces shine with happiness. These children were fortunate, and they knew it. Although most deaf and mute persons at that time were kept at home or confined to institutions, these children came mostly from well-to-do Boston families, with parents broad-minded enough or optimistic enough to believe that their conditions could improve. One reason for that optimism was the presence of Alexander Graham Bell.

Bell stands at the top of the stairs, at the extreme right. His dark hair blends into the building, so we cannot distinguish all of his features, but it is enough to see that he was a rather tall, well-built young man who wore a suit and tie, as was customary at the time for all Bostonians who did not perform manual labor. Although his serious expression makes him seem older, at the time of the photo, Bell was only 24. For the past two months he had delighted and amazed people as different as Dexter King and Sarah Fuller with his new methods for teaching the deaf, which he called *Visible Speech*.

Just as the children did, Bell looked forward to going home. His parents lived in Brantford, a town in Ontario, Canada, on the other side of Niagara Falls, and he was ready for a vacation. This had been his first teaching appointment in an American

The teachers and students of the Boston School for Deaf Mutes in Boston, Massachusetts, pose for an end-of-the-year picture on June 21, 1871.

school, and the Scot-turned-Canadian was eager to return home.

In this photograph, we can see many things that will influence and change Alexander Graham Bell's life. He will remember Dexter King as a model of Yankee politeness and intelligence, and Miss Sarah Fuller as an incredible teacher and personal friend (he is the colleague who wrote of her "Love, Goodness, and Firmness"). The children on the steps and on the side will always be part of his life, for despite his later invention of the telephone, five years later, Bell will always consider his primary occupation as "teacher of the deaf." The one person that will affect his future more than any other is Mary True, on the fourth row down. She would also teach Mabel Hubbard, the young girl who will one day share Bell's life and dreams.

Bridging the Great Divide

Alexander Bell turned 10 on March 3, 1857. Although he was a precocious young boy, he did not yet keep notes and diaries, so we know little of his thoughts at that time. By the time he turned 11 in 1858, he had become Alexander *Graham* Bell. Born to a family that prided itself on long and sonorous names, he felt that Alexander Bell (which was also his grandfather's name) was insufficient, so he added "Graham," the name of a family friend. Alexander Graham Bell (we will often refer to him as A.G. Bell) took his new name just a few months before a scientific event of major proportions, one that hinted at aspects of his future career in communications.

THE ATLANTIC CABLE

Americans and Britons (which include English, Irish, Welsh, and Scottish people) had long desired some type of rapid

communication across the Atlantic Ocean. The two groups of English-speaking peoples were in better contact than in the past, but it still took about 10 days for the fastest steam-powered vessel to cross the North Atlantic. In 1847, the year that Alexander Graham Bell was born, this did not seem to be terrible because Britain and America were at peace, but there were people alive on both sides of the ocean who remembered the tragic events of early 1815.

On January 8 of that year, General Andrew Jackson led his Southern militiamen to a resounding victory over British regiments that threatened the city of New Orleans. Running into a wall of musket and rifle fire, the British suffered great losses before they gave up the fight. Just about a month later (steamships were not yet in use) came the news that Great Britain and the United States had in fact signed the Peace of Ghent, in Belgium, on Christmas Eve of 1814. Fourteen short days separated the peace treaty from the Battle of New Orleans, but during those two weeks 2,000 British soldiers were killed, wounded, or missing. Happily, America and Britain have not gone to war since. The last battle of the War of 1812, and the horrific casualties involved, made many Americans and Britons think about the possibilities of overseas communications. There had to be a better way than waiting for the mail packets that traveled from Boston and New York to London and Liverpool.

Thirty years after the conclusion of the War of 1812, an American inventor came up with something that showed great potential for the future of communications. Samuel F.B. Morse, an American painter-turned-inventor who had studied abroad in his youth, patented the new telegraph in 1844. His first message consisted of the memorable words: "What hath God wrought!" The telegraph did not send voices or even words; instead, it transmitted a series of stops and starts that registered as dots and dashes, which could be translated into words at the other end (the beginning of International Morse Code). In the twenty-first century, we often underestimate how revolutionary

Alexander Graham Bell took on his middle name at the age 10, out of appreciation for a family friend. He is shown here around 1861, at the age of 14 or 15.

the telegraph truly was. Its invention made it possible to surpass the length of distance the human voice could carry as an instrument of swift communication. One trouble with the new system was its expense: An ordinary citizen could not use the telegraph; he or she had to go to the local telegraph office and pay an operator to send a telegram.

Even so, the telegraph took off rapidly. The United States was in the lead, but England, Germany, and France were not far behind. In these European nations, the national governments tended to make state monopolies of the telegraph, which was used for commercial, military, and diplomatic interests. England and France, which had been rivals for centuries, celebrated the laying of a cable under the English Channel, which allowed for telegraphic communication between London and Paris. There was no telegraph communication between London and Edinburgh in 1847, the year Alexander Graham Bell was born, but it came a few years later.

Successful and popular though the telegraph was, skeptics doubted it could ever bridge the great gap between Canada and the United States on one side and England, Ireland, Scotland, and Wales on the other. The distance was too great, most people agreed, and even if such a cable could be laid, it would surely be eaten by the numerous sea creatures that frequented those cold and dark waters. Cyrus West Field proved them wrong.

Born in Massachusetts in 1819, Field came from a remarkable family that included merchants, lawyers, theorists, visionaries, and even a member of the U.S. Supreme Court. By the 1850s, Cyrus Field was already a very successful businessman who lived in New York City. Excited by the idea of an undersea telegraph cable, he promoted the idea and accepted contributions from all sorts of individuals, institutions, and governments, including the U.S. Congress and the British Parliament.

By the end of 1857, when Alexander Bell was 10, Field had two warships (one British and the other American) laying an

Samuel F.B. Morse (1791–1872), shown above, invented the telegraph in the mid-nineteenth century.

enormous 2,000-mile (3,219-kilometer) cable between New-foundland's east coast and Ireland's western one. The crews and technicians had a difficult time laying the cable, running into obstacles time and again. Toward the beginning of August 1858—by which time Alexander Bell had become Alexander Graham Bell—their task was complete: The giant cable was on the ocean floor, ready for the first transmission. Victoria, the queen of Britain, sent the first message across the Atlantic: "To the Honorable president of the United States. Her Majesty desires to congratulate the president upon the successful completion of this great international work in which the Queen has taken the deepest interest."[1]

President Buchanan, who had taken office a year and a half earlier, replied,

> The president cordially reciprocates the congratulations of her Majesty, the Queen, on the success of the great international enterprise accomplished by the science, skill, and indomitable energy of the two countries. It is a triumph more glorious, because far more useful to mankind, than war ever won by conqueror on the field of battle.
>
> May the Atlantic telegraph under the blessing of heaven prove to be a bond of perpetual peace and friendship between the kindred nations, and an estimate, destined by divine Providence to dice used religion, civilization, liberty and law throughout the world. In this view will not all nations of Christendom spontaneously unite in the declaration that it shall for ever been neutral, and that its communications shall be held sacred in passing to their places of destination, even in the midst of hostilities? (signed). James Buchanan.[2]

The Queen did not immediately reply; it seemed as if there was plenty of time to do so. Just a few days later, after only a few hundred messages had been tapped out in the Morse code,

This photograph from 1920 shows a female telegraph operator typing at her machine. Telegrams remained a popular form of communication into the first half of the twentieth century.

the Atlantic cable went dead. Some time passed before engineers discerned that the difficulty was in the wiring and that an entirely new cable would be necessary. By then, tensions between the North and South in the United States had grown to extremes. The American government was not ready to commit any money or energy to a new Atlantic telegraph, and the communications of North America and Europe, successful for a few days, were severed yet again for the space of nine years.

No one knows how Alexander Graham Bell felt about the failure of the Atlantic telegraph. We are certain, though, that he was already starting to tune in, to however small a degree, to the work that would occupy his life: the annihilation of distance through the transmission of sound.

The Power
of Family

"Do something useful."
—Mr. Herdman, the father of
A.G. Bell's friend, speaking to the two boys

In the previous chapter we noted that Cyrus West Field, promoter of the Atlantic telegraph, came from a remarkable family. The same can be said of Alexander Graham Bell.

Bell's paternal grandfather, Alexander Bell Sr., was born in Scotland in 1790. The son of a cobbler, he followed his father's trade for a time before he turned to the stage. Blessed with a remarkably strong voice, Alexander Bell combined acting with teaching elocution at several schools in Edinburgh, Scotland's intellectual and political capital. He prospered until his late thirties, when he found out that his wife of more than a decade was having an affair. The ensuing lawsuit harmed Alexander

Bell's reputation and cost him most of the money he had made in his life. Because he needed a change, he moved to London and continued to teach elocution.

Elocution, though often confused with oratory or rhetoric, is a more exact science. A professional elocutionist (the word entered the English language in 1847) must come to know both the inner aspects of speech, such as the lungs and vocal chords, as well as the outer ones, such as dialect and facial expression. Oratory and rhetoric had been around since the time of the Romans and Greeks, but elocution was a fairly new discipline when Alexander Bell turned in that direction. It can still be debated whether it is an art or a science.

Alexander Bell brought David and Alexander, his two eldest sons, to London with him, but they were soon off to other parts of the English-speaking world. Both sons had spent some time in Canada for health reasons, and both were convinced that the bracing climate of the New World was good for body and soul. David Bell returned to Europe to take up residence in Dublin, where he became a famed elocutionist (the playwright George Bernard Shaw once called him the most impressive, majestic man he had ever known), and Alexander moved to Edinburgh, where he had been born.

FATHER BELL

Born in Edinburgh in 1819, Alexander Melville Bell was best known as Melville. Blessed with rich black hair and a strong physique, he had many of his father's attributes, and it was no surprise that he turned to the work of elocution. In 1844, he met and married Eliza Grace Symonds. The daughter of a British naval officer, she was almost 10 years older than her husband, but the age difference did not harm the marriage in the least. Neither did her deafness.

Hard of hearing from her early years, Eliza Symonds (now Eliza Bell) used an ear trumpet but still heard only very little. Remarkably, her handicap did not prevent her from learn-ing and playing the piano: She held her ear trumpet to the

Alexander Melville Bell is pictured here in 1884 with his wife, Eliza Grace Symonds, and their granddaughter Elsie May Bell at Beinn Bhreagh, Nova Scotia.

keyboard and played beautifully. Eliza and Melville appeared to be made for each other, and their 52 years together revealed few disappointments. Theirs was a singularly happy marriage.

BROTHERS

A.G. Bell, as we shall call Alexander Graham to avoid confusion with his many relatives, was the second of three boys in the family. Melville James Bell (called Melly), born in 1845, was his elder brother and Edward Charles Bell (called Ted), born in 1848, was his younger sibling.

EARLY YEARS

We know a good deal about A.G.'s youth because his parents were note-keepers and letter writers. In addition, the art of photography blossomed in the 1850s, and Melville Bell, an enthusiastic photographer, left us a set of visual cues as to what his son's life was like.

Melville Bell was at the peak of his physical prowess during the 1850s, and he seemed like a giant to his rather shy middle son. A.G. was somewhat afraid and overwhelmed by his august father, but Melville and his eldest son, Melly, delighted in each other's company. A.G. was much closer with his mother, Eliza Symonds Bell, who was both gracious and cheerful most of the time. A fine musician in her own right, she hired an impressive tutor for her middle son, and his earliest happy memories had to do with playing the piano. Mother and middle son also bonded in that he alone, of all the family, could whisper around her forehead in such a way that she could hear.

Younger brother Ted and A.G. were also close. They shared a gentle nature and a desire for privacy, something foreign to their outspoken, brash elder brother. Photographs from the 1850s usually show A.G. and his brother Ted together, with Melville Bell and Melly acting as a pair. There might have been serious strain in the family affections if Eliza Symonds Bell had not held everyone close and dear to her heart: She was the feminine glue that held the masculine Bells together.

As mentioned in the previous chapter, we have no knowledge of A.G. Bell's reaction to the first Atlantic telegraph cable, laid in 1858. We are confident, however, that he was already thinking in terms of invention.

THE FIRST ATTEMPT

"Invention is," as Thomas Edison later said, "2 percent inspiration and 98 percent perspiration."

A.G. Bell found this out sometime around the age of 10 or 11, when he and a friend tried to follow the friend's father's advice to "do something useful." His friend's father owned a mill. One day, irritated by the boys' constant play, he challenged them to do something about the husks of grain that naturally stuck to an ear of corn. Bell's friend passed this task off lightly, but Bell spent a few days on it, and he came up with a primitive sort of motor-driven instrument that would indeed strip the husks from the corn. Amazed, his friend's father used it in the mill. Years later, Bell recalled, "So far as I remember, Mr. Herdman's injunction to do something useful was my first incentive to invention, and the method of cleaning wheat the first fruit."[1]

Still, no one expected any of the Bell brothers to do very much with their hands in the future. All three boys had talent—that was clear enough—but it lay in their brains and their voices. Trained by their elocutionist father, all three boys developed wonderful voices from an early age. Although they became proficient in imitating all sorts of accents, they actually specialized in clear, resonant production of the King's, or Queen's, English.

SCHOOLING

All three boys went to Kings High School in Edinburgh. Melly, the eldest, was the best by far, winning honors in languages and vocabulary, but A.G. and his brother Ted were close to the bottom of their classes. The reason certainly was not ability; perhaps it was that these two boys, rather dreamy by nature, had become accustomed to tuning out much of what adults told them. At any rate, Melville and Eliza Bell decided their sons needed a little shaking up, so in 1862, A.G. learned he was to leave for London to serve as a companion and helper to his grandfather.

Many years had passed since the cobbler had become an actor, but the senior Alexander Bell remained a formidable presence. A square-set, fine-looking man late in life, Grandfather Bell had known plenty of adversity, including his painful divorce, along the way. When his middle grandson arrived by train in 1863, Grandfather Bell promptly announced that he needed a whole new wardrobe; his clothes might be appropriate for Edinburgh, but they would not do in the British capital.

Accustomed to an almost rural lifestyle (the Bells had always spent some time outside of Edinburgh) A.G. felt rather cloistered at the beginning of his London stay. His grandfather did not walk that much, and the two Bells—separated by almost 60 years—were strangers at first, but that feeling soon passed. Grandfather Bell was a master at training young men, and he had been doing so for more than 40 years. Within a few months of his arrival, A.G. looked and acted like a new person; the teenager looked almost like a man. The casual clothes of Edinburgh and the countryside were gone, replaced by elegant ones and a new, more sophisticated, attitude. Like almost all Londoners, A.G. soon wore a hat on all occasions, and he began to look and act older than his 16 years. More important, he learned specifics from his grandfather about elocution, especially how to help stammerers to overcome their disability.

Back in Scotland, Melville Bell did not know how much his son had changed, but he wrote an earnest letter: "We miss you sadly when we assemble by the fireside at the cottage, but we are reconciled to your absence by the fact that you are good to Grandpa and have been a great comfort to him in his illness. . . . You will have cause of thankfulness all your life that you had the benefit of such a training as my father has lovingly afforded you."[2] Melville wrote from experience; he had received that same training many years ago. Even so, he was somewhat astonished when a polished, precise-speaking, impeccably dressed young man came home. One year in London, and the company of his grandfather, had done wonders for Alexander Graham Bell.

PROFESSIONAL DEVELOPMENT

A.G. was only 17 when he returned from the big city, but he was ready for bigger tasks. When Melville realized that Melly

Alexander Bell Sr., grandfather of Alexander Graham Bell, is shown in this photograph, which was taken between 1850 and 1859.

and A.G. both needed new challenges, he suggested they try to build a replica of human speech—in other words, a talking device.

Rising to the challenge, Melly and A.G. worked for weeks to build the replica of the upper part of the human body. The brothers knew a lot about the larynx, pharynx, and vocal cords already, but the work made them more expert than before. When they finished, the brothers had concocted a device that could indeed utter a few sounds when the boys breathed air into its lungs. Because the brothers found it easiest, as babies do, to make the sound "Ah," a neighbor came downstairs to ask what was wrong with the baby.

Melly and A.G. became closer than ever before. They shared, along with all the male Bells, a profound interest in the workings of human speech, and A.G. had matured so much in the past year and a half that he and Melly now became quite companionable. Soon they even applied for the same type of job, as teachers of elocution in private secondary schools. Learning of this, Melville Bell worked out an arrangement under which Melly would attend university for one year while A.G. taught at a private school, with the understanding that the two brothers would switch positions in the following year. So it was that A.G., at the tender age of 17, began to teach high school boys, a few of whom were actually older than he was.

The work was at Elgin School in the extreme northeast part of Scotland. The distant, even remote, quality of the landscape might have daunted some young men, but A.G. was thrilled with it. Always a hiking enthusiast, he got into some scrapes and minor dangers, but generally he loved his first year of teaching. In his spare time, A.G. experimented with tonal qualities; a roommate sometimes found him up in the middle of the night, gently pressuring different parts of his throat to test the quality of the vocal chords. Another person might have been labeled an eccentric, but A.G. already had a winning, disarming quality that won him many friends and very few enemies. His dedication to teaching and to his own learning was evident.

FATHER'S TRIUMPH

Grandfather Bell died in the spring of 1865, at the age of 75. Melville and Eliza Bell quickly moved from Edinburgh to

London, where they took over Grandfather Bell's house and his elocution practice. If Melville Bell seemed to be ascending in the world through his father's labors, the appearance was false; he was in fact, on the threshold of a very grand achievement that was all his own.

Sometime in the late 1840s, Melville Bell had conceived the idea of a universal alphabet, one based on a set of universal sounds. Many phoneticians had thought of this, and quite a few had tried, but virtually all had given up in exasperation. Melville Bell had the patience, the knowledge, and the sheer grit to keep at the task, year after year, even while he kept up his regular teaching work. (He passed this ability to work late into the night onto his son A.G.). Although almost two decades passed between the conception and the delivery, Grandfather Bell was fortunate to live long enough to know that the great work was near completion. In 1867, Melville Bell's *Visible Speech: The Science of Universal Alphabetics* was published in London.

After describing the elements that go into the making of speech (larynx, pharynx, soft palate, tongue, and lips), Melville listed the different potential applications of his system of Visible Speech. It could, he wrote, aid in:

Teaching the illiterate
Teaching the blind to read
Teaching the deaf and dumb to speak
Helping people pronounce words in foreign languages
Establishing a universal pronunciation standard
Removing impediments, such as stammering, and
The telegraphic communication of messages in
    any language, through all countries, without
    translation.[3]

Not everyone who read *Visible Speech* thought that it would help in all these capacities, but most trained elocutionists agreed that it had significant potential. Melville Bell had done

[ENGLISH ALPHABET OF VISIBLE SPEECH,

Expressed in the Names of Numbers and Objects.]

[EXERCISE.]

One by one.

Two or three.

Four at once.

Five o'clock.

Half-past six.

Seven-thirty.

Eight to nine.

Ten or twelve.

Twice two, four.

Twice three, six.

Four and four, eight.

Nine and two, eleven.

Twice or thrice.

Two, a couple.

Twelve, a dozen.

Twenty, a score.

A book-case.

A few books.

New book-shelves.

A silver watch.

A gold watch.

The watch-key.

A good saw.

Cap and feather.

Tongs and shovel.

Sugar-tongs.

A hunting whip.

A table lamp.

A bunch of onions.

Corns and bunions.

A ship's boat.

A sailing boat.

Cart and horse.

A round tent.

Rows of houses.

A dog-kennel.

A little monkey.

A pretty cage.

A green canary.

In the late 1840s, Melville Bell conceived the idea of a universal alphabet based on a set of universal sounds. In 1867, his *Visible Speech: The Science of Universal Alphabetics* was published in London. This is a chart illustrating the symbols he used.

the world a great service, one that would require extensive training for those who wished to use it. As an attempt to counteract this claim, Melville asked his sons to demonstrate how it might be used. The three sons would leave the room, during which time a skilled elocutionist or professor of languages would make a number of challenging accents and sounds, such as the Cockney dialect or something from a Native American language. Melville would then write the sound or its representation in his new Visible Speech characters, and when they returned, his sons would invariably be able to pronounce the difficult words and phrases without any training or prompting. One hardly needs to point out, however, that the Bell sons were extremely proficient readers and enunciators, and it was possible that other persons might have had a difficult time replicating their success.

As in the past, A.G. was undoubtedly a bit overwhelmed by his father's stupendous success, but there was some consolation. Toward the very end of the work, Melville inserted the use of Visible Speech in the translation of Zulu clicks, as performed by his son; this was the first time Alexander Graham Bell was cited in a professional work.

Melville Bell did not make very much money from Visible Speech. Neither the British government nor the British public was ready for this type of transition. He did, however, acquire lasting fame and enough money that he could feel freer to pursue an old goal.

While both Melville and his brother David Bell had spent some time in Canada in their youth, David admitted that even as a boy he was most inclined toward the "stars and stripes" as a symbol of freedom in the world. Visible Speech became their ticket to America, and it served as the launching pad for Alexander Graham Bell, who was fast following in their footsteps.

The Lure
of America

"Entering the States, even from Canada, is like pushing out from a sheltered creek into the current. Almost immediately you feel the catch of a swifter life."
—*A comment made by one of Melville Bell's students*

At about the same time that Melville Bell was achieving the culmination of his professional, if not monetary, dreams, Alexander Graham Bell was at the beginning of his own. He had no way of knowing how far his early experiments would take him in the next decade, but he may have sensed that, like his father, his work would take a long time to unfold.

TUNING FORKS

A.G. had always possessed an exceptionally keen ear. Sometime in 1866 he started to play with tuning forks, hoping he could transmit sound over a short distance. This naturally led him to the realm of electricity, one of the most burgeoning fields of the time.

Like his father, Bell was fascinated with all aspects of speech, and father and son collaborated in one important discovery: While listening to a scale of musical notes, Melville thought they were in an ascending scale and A.G. thought the reverse. At first they tangled, much like in earlier times, but then they came to the startling conclusion that the vowel sounds actually had *two* pitches, one ascending and the other descending.

Making his first battery and motor, A.G. worked with tuning forks. His aim was to tune them so finely that they would only receive and imitate the precise sound that they themselves produced. A.G. may not have known it then, but he was in the very early stages of working on what was later called the harmonic telegraph.

Telegraphy, or the sending of telegraph messages, was only about 20 years old in 1867. The telegraph had already proved to be one of the marvelous developments of the age of invention in the nineteenth century. There was some frustration, however, about the type of messages that could be sent, as well as the hindrance of having only one telegraph wire. In 1867, operators could send only one message at a time. A.G. was beginning work that he hoped would someday make it possible to send a number of messages simultaneously: The transmitter and receiver would be so finely tuned, acoustically speaking, that they would only respond to messages sent by their exact counterpart.

A.G. wrote excitedly to Alexander Ellis, London's foremost acoustic expert, who wrote back, saying that A.G. had independently discovered what the German scientist Helmholtz had found a few years earlier. Ellis later translated Helmholtz's work into English, but in the meantime, A.G. was somewhat crestfallen that his special discovery was not as novel as he had hoped. This was to be one of the themes of A.G.'s professional life: In a time when all sorts of men (and few women) aspired to be inventors, there was a constant series of hits, misses, and entanglements. One of the most striking evidences of this came a decade later (see Chapter 6).

TRAGEDY

Ted Bell, the youngest of the three brothers, died in 1867. The gentlest and happiest of the boys, he had been the heart of the family, much as their mother still was. Tuberculosis—that great nineteenth-century killer—was the culprit.

Melly Bell, eldest of the three brothers, married in that same year. He soon had a son, but that boy was born weak and died 18 months later. It seemed that tragedy surrounded the Bell family.

In the nineteenth century, people did not ascribe such disasters to bad luck or misfortune; they took for granted that life was dangerous and that disease abounded. Science was making remarkable strides in that century, but medical knowledge had not yet made the same inroads, and a vaccine for tuberculosis was still years away.

Then, as if there was no end to the run of tragic loss, Melly Bell came down with tuberculosis. He died in the spring of 1870, leaving his widow, Carrie Bell, but no children.

Melville and Eliza Bell had spent the better part of their lives as parents of three boys, two of whom had been ripped from them. Desperate to preserve the health of their one remaining son, they asked A.G. and his sister-in-law Carrie to emigrate with them to Canada. A.G. had many conflicting feelings on the matter: He felt that he was making headway with his studies and his amateur invention, and had been courting a young woman, so he did not wish to leave for Canada. One evening, after taking a long walk, he returned to find his mother and father in the living room, quiet and expectant, hoping he would agree.

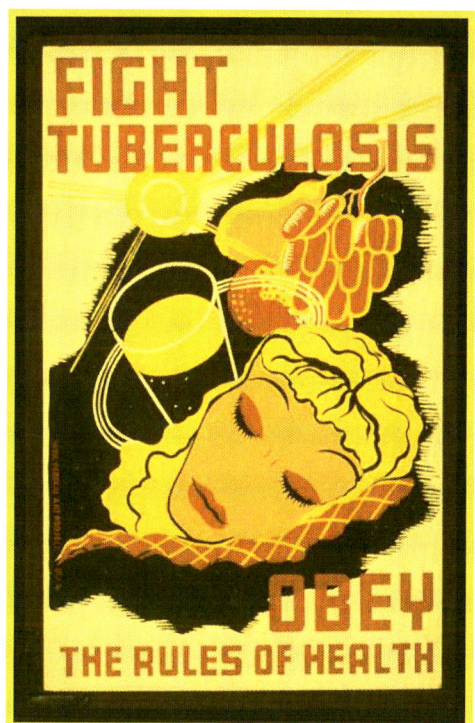

This government poster from the late 1930s promotes the prevention of tuberculosis with illustrations of better eating and sleeping habits, and more exposure to sunshine. At the time that this disease killed Ted Bell in 1867, it was a leading cause of death.

The moment was poignant. At 22, A.G. was eager to be on his own, but his parents' obvious desire won him over. In typical Bell fashion, he left a letter for posterity:

> The dream that you know I have cherished for so long has *perished* with poor Melly. . . . Do not think me ungrateful because I have been unhappy at home for the last two years. I have now no other wish than to be with you, Mama, and Carrie, and I put myself unreservedly into your hands to do with me whatever you think for the best. I am, dear Papa, Your affectionate and *only* son, Aleck.[1]

The dream that perished with his brother is uncertain to us today. Did he mean an academic partnership with Melly? Did he mean his affections for the young woman mentioned above?

We cannot say, but the son's letter to the father stands as a fine record of the filial piety that Victorian society encouraged. One did not live only for oneself; one also lived for others. The Bells left for Canada in the summer of 1870.

THE NEW WORLD

On the crossing from England to Canada, A.G. wrote in his journal that he was now a man, and that he would depend entirely on his own opinions of matters and situations. Perhaps he regretted giving in to his parents' need for his company, but it was too late to turn back now.

After they reached Quebec, the Bells paused briefly in Montreal and then settled in Ontario. About 45 miles (72.4 kilometers) west of Niagara Falls they found and purchased a nice country home for $2,600 (this was at a time when a laborer would make $500 per year). Melville Bell left, almost immediately, for a lecture tour throughout part of the United States to demonstrate Visible Speech, while A.G. remained at the new family home. If he had been in danger of contracting tuberculosis as his parents had always feared, A.G. would have quickly recovered. That autumn he picked apples, took long hikes, and even spent some time with the Mohawk tribe, transcribing some of their language into Visible Speech.

Melville Bell and his brother David loved America. One of Melville's students, who wrote a book about America, had this to say: "Entering the States, even from Canada, is like pushing out from a sheltered creek into the current. Almost immediately you feel the catch of a swifter life. . . . The climate has something to do with all this. Even the passing traveler soon becomes conscious of the influence of that intensely clear vivifying atmosphere."[2] Not that the United States was all wine and roses. Rather, the student wrote, America was vivifying because of the extremes of heat and cold, as well as the difficulties of everyday life. Americans, he said, were rising to the challenges presented by their immense continent, and they had much to offer Europe.

While he was in Boston, Melville Bell met Sarah Fuller, the principal of a new school for the deaf and mute. A middle-aged woman of great charm and skill, she asked the creator of Visible Speech if he would become the school's elocution teacher, but he replied that he had spent 20 years creating Visible Speech and did not wish to spend the next 20 teaching it. One conversation led to another; before long, A.G. learned of this opportunity. Although he was still in Ontario, he could go to Boston to teach the young charges of Miss Fuller's school.

In early April 1871, A.G. arrived in Boston for the first time. Within just a few days he met most of the leading speech teachers in the city and had received invitations to lectures at the Massachusetts Institute of Technology (MIT). Possessed of great mental and physical energy, A.G. made a positive impression on nearly everyone he encountered.

When he first appeared at Sarah Fuller's school, A.G. made an even greater impression. Not quiet and shy as he sometimes was in private, in the classroom he held forth like everyone's favorite uncle: Most of the students did not guess he was only 24. Using his father's techniques of Visible Speech, A.G. drew pictures of the mouth, throat, and lungs on the blackboard, and he soon had his impressionable students pointing to the corresponding anatomical parts of their own bodies. Within days, some of the students, who may have been considered hopeless, began to speak.

It is not too much to say that A.G. was a sensation that spring. Middle- and upper-class Bostonians quickly learned of this enterprising and gifted teacher who made such a difference with his young charges. In nineteenth-century America, as well as in Europe, deafness was more common than today. In part because of the prevalence of scarlet fever, for which there were

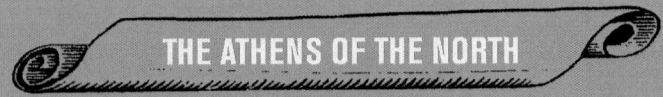

THE ATHENS OF THE NORTH

Alexander Graham Bell had grown up in Edinburgh, Scotland, which was then known as the Athens of the North. Scots led the way in philosophy, engineering, and many of the sciences. By 1871, the year he came to Boston, this American city was close to supplanting the Scottish one as an intellectual and artistic center.

First settled in 1630, Boston had long been the center of American religion, culture, and politics. Although New York had become the nation's business capital, and Washington D.C. had become the political capital, Boston was almost giddily supreme in the arts and sciences in 1871. No other American city boasted so large a public library, so many charitable and benevolent institutions, or so many artists, scientists, writers, and philosophers. A.G. had unknowingly come to precisely the right place to conduct his future scientific experiments.

Of course, no rose is ever without its thorns, and Boston had its share. Though the city had played a marked role in the abolitionist movement, blacks and whites were effectively segregated. There was, if anything, an even greater prejudice against Boston's large Irish community, most of whom had arrived after the Potato Famine of 1845. Catholics were still referred to as Papists in 1870s Boston, and a severe line was drawn between recent Celtic immigrants (the Irish) and earlier Anglo-Saxon ones (the Puritans who had come in the 1600s).

A.G. experienced almost no prejudice or separation from Boston's high society, however. As a recent Scottish immigrant to Canada, he came from a society similar, in many ways, to Boston's, and he spoke a highly refined version of the King's English. Like many other foreign travelers of the time, he marveled at American hospitality: Americans, he wrote, did not seem to know the meaning of want. That was true for the upper class that he came to know, but it was quite untrue for untold thousands who labored in the nearby sweatshops of Chelsea, Revere, and Cambridge.

Sarah Fuller sits at the front of her class while a pupil writes on the board at the Horace Mann School for the Deaf in 1893.

no antibiotics, deafness struck without regard for social class or rank, and many imposing men of society had a deaf son or daughter. Without expecting it, A.G. had stumbled into an area of real fortune.

Memorable
Meetings

"I did not like him."
—*Mabel Hubbard's first impression of A. G. Bell*

Before he reached Brantford, Ontario, which had become home, Alexander Graham Bell met a man whose future career would be inextricably combined with his own. Twenty-six years older than Bell, and a bit taller and thinner, Gardiner Greene Hubbard was the essence of Yankee skill and ingenuity. Earning a bachelor's degree from Dartmouth was only the first of his many accomplishments, which included graduating from Harvard Law School. He had recently become embroiled in a legal and legislative conflict with Western Union, the company that exercised a virtual monopoly over telegraphic communications in America. The conversations between Bell and Hubbard did not begin with telegraphy, or even with the primitive idea of the telephone, but rather with deaf and mute children. Hubbard had founded the Clarke School for the Deaf in Northampton, Massachusetts, and he was eager for Bell to observe the teaching methods practiced there.

SUCCESS

Bell had gained much from his first year in America. In 1870, he had crossed the ocean as a rather unknown quantity; by the summer of 1871, he was a sought-after teacher, one who was greatly respected, at least where teaching the deaf was concerned. Bell did let his success go to his head sometimes, but his father would remind him of how much he had to learn. Relations between father and son remained difficult in many ways, but Bell proved to be a truly loyal son. Although many schools and principals were now interested in what he had to offer, he always deferred to his father's system of Visible Speech as the answer to their problems. Of course, he was the best man to present that system to them.

In his second year of teaching in Boston, Bell met a five-year-old boy, Georgie Sanders, whose life would also be intertwined with his own. The son of a prosperous Salem merchant, Sanders had been deaf since birth, unlike Bell's other deaf students, which presented greater challenges to Bell and to the system of Visible Speech. Far from shrinking from the challenge, Bell accepted it. He soon moved to the boy's grandmother's home in Salem to become his permanent tutor.

NEW METHODS

Bell was already a very skillful teacher, but he adopted new methods to teach Georgie Sanders. Sometimes Bell wrote alphabet letters on gloves, which both he and Georgie wore, and sometimes he went to great lengths to demonstrate the meaning of words and phrases. Both pupil and teacher

Gardiner Greene Hubbard is shown reading in his study. Hubbard would become a major presence in Bell's life, especially after Bell married Hubbard's daughter, Mabel.

alike benefitted from this situation: Georgie had a patient, adoring instructor, and Bell received free room and board at the Sanders home. Within a year, Georgie's grandmother offered Bell another room in her house, this one to be used as a study. That was fortunate for Bell for he was onto something quite new.

THE HARMONIC TELEGRAPH

As mentioned in Chapter 3, Bell had first visualized the harmonic telegraph as early as 1867, but he did not have much chance to work on it until about 1872 or 1873. It is hard to say just what moment or situation inspired him; perhaps it is safer to say that he never forgot his interest in the telegraphic transmission of musical notes, and that he was encouraged by some of his early findings.

By the beginning of 1873, Bell had started to work in earnest. How he managed to fit study and experiment time into his already busy schedule remains one of the mysteries of his life. Although Bell had plenty of nervous and intellectual energy, he still had to eat, sleep, and rest on occasion. He stayed up until about 1:00 A.M., and then slept very soundly (friends complained it was impossible to awaken him) until about 9:00 in the mornings.

Bell was still fixed on the idea of transmitting musical notes as a precursor to transmitting a number of messages, simultaneously, over the same telegraph line. To illustrate his idea, Bell performed an old piano trick, in which he sang into a piano until a key struck a note on its own. Many observers came away unconvinced, he kept at it just the same.

Never having taken even a rudimentary course in electricity, Bell had to play with batteries, acid, mercury, and the like on his own. This suited his temperament quite well, and by the end of 1873, he knew as much about these materials as did the average electrician. Still, he needed more specialized hands to perform the involved work, and he found these in the man who would become his great friend and assistant, Thomas A. Watson.

THE NEW PARTNERSHIP

Years later, speaking to a group of communication enthusiasts known as the Telephone Pioneers, Watson recalled his first meeting with the man who would change his life: "One day when I was hard at work on it [a torpedo-exploding apparatus], a tall, slender, quick-motioned man with pale face, black side whiskers, and drooping moustache, big nose and high sloping forehead crowned with bushy jet black hair, came rushing out of the office and over to my work bench."[1]

Eighteen-year-old Watson had worked in Charles Williams's Electrical Shop in Boston for the past three years. Born to a poor family in Salem, he had dropped out of school at 13 and tried several types of work before he found the Williams workshop, which performed all sorts of tests and made various mechanical objects, many of them for would-be inventors. Most of these men had wealthy sponsors ready to hand out money so they could indulge their pet projects. Young as he was, Watson quietly looked down on many of these men, but he saw very quickly that Alexander Graham Bell was something different: a man quite in earnest.

ELECTRICITY

The telephone, as devised by Alexander Graham Bell, employs electricity to send signals, which are then replicated at the other end of the line. How did Bell, who was not trained as an electrician or even as a scientist, come to unravel such mysteries of the natural world?

Electricity comes from the Greek *electron*, which means "amber." The ancient Greeks observed natural electricity and found that amber was one of the best conductors.

Benjamin Franklin, in addition to being one of America's Founding Fathers, was also one of the earliest to experiment with electricity. His famous kite experiments showed that electricity was a natural phenomenon, but it also suggested that humans could tinker with it and perhaps bring it into alignment with their own purposes.

The Italian scientist Alessandro Volta, after whom the word *volt* is named, is credited with being the first to explain certain aspects of electricity. The Englishman Michael Farraday went further in the 1820s and 1830s, but there was still much that was unknown, especially how electricity could be harnessed.

Bell told Watson that an instrument he had designed had not been made according to specification, and he went on to describe what his multiple, or harmonic, telegraph would be like. Watson recalled it:

> There were, say, six transmitters with their springs tuned to six different pitches and six receivers with their springs tuned to correspond. Now, theoretically, when a transmitter sent its electrical whine into the line wire, its own

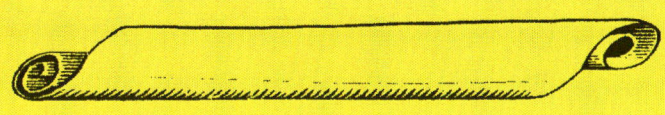

Electricity was the power behind the telegraph, so it followed that electricity also supported the telephone. There were plenty of times along the way, however, when Bell and other inventors worked in the dark. Bell made one of his breakthroughs in 1867 with his tuning forks, and another in 1873 when he began to pursue the electric transmission of speech in earnest. One great moment came in 1875 when he realized that the electric current in a wire would reflect the impressions made on it by signals at the transmitter end. Bell did not know how strong those transmissions had to be, and in the early days of experimentation he usually shouted, rather than whispered, into his devices. Only gradually did he learn how exquisitely malleable electricity is, how its current could be influenced by even the slightest variation in transmission. In this, electricity resembled the human ear, which is adept at catching all sorts of sounds.

There were still questions to be answered, and there are still questions, even today. Bell, who was not trained in the sciences, used his intuition and day-by-day experimentation to arrive at results denied to men of greater scientific knowledge.

Thomas Watson holds a model of Alexander Graham Bell's first telephone. Watson worked for three years at an electrical shop in Boston before he met Bell at the age of 18.

faithful receiver spring at the distant station would wriggle sympathetically but all the others on the same line would remain coldly quiescent. . . . One wire would do the work of six, and the "Duplex" telegraph that had just been invented would be beaten to a frazzle.[2]

A number of competitors were working on this. Bell, however, was in the lead in some respects, largely because of his knowledge of acoustics. Watson did not come to work with Bell until a bit later, but he became Bell's "go-to" man in the Williams workshop, and these men from very different backgrounds struck up a lively friendship.

USING THE EAR

By the time he met Watson, Bell had already begun one of his most important experiments. Using a human ear from a cadaver, supplied to him by a friend in the medical profession, Bell constructed a phonautograph. When he attached a tiny piece of chalk to the ear membranes, then blew into the ear by means of a trumpet, he was astonished to see that the chalk made very distinct marks, which resembled waves, on paper or glass. Bell was not the first person, by any means, to experiment with sound waves, but he made the discovery largely on his own.

The more Bell thought about this, the more excited he became. If the mere activity of his breath, coming through the trumpet, could stir the ear membranes to trace little lines, then what might a voice do over wires? He was still far from the ultimate completion of his invention, but each day he came a bit closer to seeing it take shape in his mind.

Watson, who was now working with Bell in rented rooms above the Williams workshop, vividly remembered the first time Bell confided to him about his ultimate design: "If I could make a current of electricity vary in intensity, precisely as the air varies in density during the production of a sound, I should be able to transmit [human] speech telegraphically."[3] Bell sketched something on the spot, but Watson did not make it, for the instrument was too costly at the time. Although Bell had clients at home and he had received an appointment as professor of oration at Boston University, he did not have the funds required. Where was the money to come from?

MEETING MABEL

Many years later, Mabel Gardiner Hubbard described her first meeting with Bell, in 1874, at her parents' home in Cambridge, Massachusetts: "I did not like him. He was tall and dark, with jet black hair and eyes, but dressed badly and carelessly in an old-fashioned suit of black broadcloth, making his hair look shiny, and altogether, to one accustomed to the dainty neatness of Harvard students, he seemed hardly a gentleman."[4] This was one occasion where first impressions definitely did not make or break the relationship.

Born in November 1857, Mabel was ten years younger than Bell. He came to her parents' home to discuss telegraphy, as well as the possibilities of a harmonic telegraph, but he soon became Mabel's teacher. She had been deaf since the age of five as a result of scarlet fever.

Many biographers have remarked on the incredible coincidence that Bell should fall in love with the daughter of one of the few men in Boston—or anywhere else, for that matter—who could give him substantial help to develop his inventions. All the letters that passed between them (which may be viewed online through the Library of Congress), however, indicate that Bell's affection for Mabel was unselfish and genuine. Certainly it did not hurt that her father was an active attorney, who specialized in patent cases, or that the connection might in some way bring him benefit, but Bell appears to have loved Mabel for her sweet and loving nature. She did not reciprocate this love for some time to come.

This photograph of Mabel Gardiner Hubbard is from 1917. Hubbard and Bell met when Hubbard was still a child and Bell was her tutor.

A THREE-WAY PARTNERSHIP

Gardiner Greene Hubbard and Alexander Graham Bell had much in common. Both were earnest, fast-thinking men, and both were eager to promote things that would benefit the public. At the same time, both men also had eyes on the main prize: a way to become rich.

Hubbard was already quite prosperous when they met, and Bell was not, but the possibilities offered by the harmonic, or multiple, telegraph excited Hubbard. Bell reported their conversation in a long letter home to his parents:

"He called his wife and made me explain it all to her, and when she raised some objection to our point, he answered it himself saying, 'Don't you see there is only one *air* and so there need be but one *wire*.'"[5] Hubbard was catching on to the potential.

Later that year, in 1874, Bell, Hubbard, and Thomas Sanders (Georgie's father) signed papers creating a three-way partnership. The two older men would back Bell with their hard-earned dollars and he would contribute the sweat equity, laboring on the invention intended to revolutionize the practice of telegraphy.

Breakthrough

Most Americans have, at some point or another, heard of the dramatic moment in which Alexander Graham Bell called his assistant, shouting the famous words "Mr. Watson—come here—I want to see you!" The immediacy of those words suggests that the telephone was invented in a hurry, or that Bell and Watson moved quickly and smoothly to an appointed end. Nothing could be further from the truth.

COMPETITION

Sometime in 1874, Bell became aware of the man who was his closest competitor in the race to create a harmonic, or multiple, telegraph. Born in Ohio in 1835, Elisha Gray had experienced a difficult time in life. He had tried a number of professions, including carpentry, before he found that he was physically unsuited for most of them. As a student at Oberlin

College in his late twenties, Gray discovered a real talent for all things electric. He obtained his first patent in 1867, and by the time he and Bell entered the race to create the harmonic telegraph, Gray was much better known than Bell.

In 1872, Gray and some of his associates created Western Electric Manufacturing Company, centered in Chicago, and he therefore had access to more skilled craftsmen than did Bell. More important, Gray knew a great deal more about electricity, both the theory and the practical applications. When he became aware of his competitor in 1874, Bell keenly desired to be first in line, as well as first to the patent office. He could not do this without the assistance of Gardiner Greene Hubbard.

Trained in the law and a specialist in patents, Hubbard had Bell send him a number of signed, sealed, and postdated memorandums, each of which had some bearing on the progress of invention. From long experience, Hubbard knew that Bell must be able to demonstrate the primacy of his idea, as well as the primacy of the actual patent date. What Hubbard did not realize—not until the moment it was made public—was Bell's increasing romantic interest in his daughter.

Mabel Hubbard, about to turn 17, was also unaware of her speech tutor's interest. She and her friends thought Bell, to be at least eight years older than his true age of 27. (He had appeared to be older than his years ever since his apprenticeship under Grandfather Bell in London.) Bell kept his feelings secret until the early summer of 1875, although they seemed ready to burst within him.

At the same time, the work on the harmonic telegraph proceeded rapidly. Bell had hired Thomas Watson away from the Williams workshop, and the two men were working upstairs in the same building, in rented rooms. Day by day they experimented with sulphur, mercury, iron, and the like. Sometimes they seemed close to creating the harmonic telegraph, and sometimes they seemed as far off as ever.

This 1879 wood engraving shows Elisha Gray, Bell's primary competitor in the race to the development of a harmonic telegraph. In fact, before Bell was granted a patent, Gray was the better known of the two inventors.

THE SMITHSONIAN

In March 1875, Bell went to Washington, D.C., both to examine the possibility of patents and to meet Professor Joseph Henry, the first secretary of the Smithsonian Institution. Henry had been experimenting for 50 years, and he had been involved in the creation of the telegraph. Even Bell, with his knowledge of the scientific world, did not understand quite how eminent Henry was. At first the conversation seemed routine, but when Bell said he had enjoyed some success using an induction coil to stir electricity in a wire, Henry showed great interest. Bell returned the next day with his materials, and the 80-year-old observed the 27-year-old at work. Bell said, "I sat at the instrument working and he sat at a table for a long time with the empty coil of wire against his ear listening to the sound."[1] Henry and Bell then discussed the best way to bring this new invention to the public.

"He said he thought it was 'the germ of a great invention'—and advised me to work at it myself instead of publishing."[2] Bell replied that he believed he did not have the technical expertise in electricity to solve the problem, to which the aged professor responded "Get it!"[3] The reply heartened Bell, who redoubled his efforts.

JUNE

The first month of summer is often magical, but that of 1875 proved especially important to Bell, both in his personal and professional life. The second day of June proved inordinately hot, and Bell was extremely susceptible to heat. He and Watson got together just the same and worked through the morning to the middle of the afternoon. Watson later described what happened:

> We were in the attic hard at work experimenting with renewed enthusiasm over some improved piece of the

apparatus. About the middle of the afternoon we were re-tuning the receiver reeds [metal discs], Bell in one room pressing the reeds against his ear one by one as I sent him the intermittent current from the other room. One of my transmitter reeds stopped vibrating. I plucked it with my fingers to start it going. The contact point was evidently screwed too hard against the reed and I began to readjust the screw while

THE EQUIPMENT

Today, with our cell phones, pagers, and the like, it is difficult to understand how primitive the materials were that Bell and Watson used in 1875.

Bell and Watson understood many of the principles of electricity. From the beginning, they had fashioned devices with both transmitters and receivers, although for a long time they used the same handle both to listen and to speak. Both men were natural experimenters, so they used different liquids for conduction and different metals to supply the electrical current. On June 2, 1875, that magical day of first transmission, Watson was tightening a steel reed, or metal disc, which was meant to "play" sound in much the same way as the later phonograph. That first sound, the twang of June 2, was nothing more than the transmission of a steel reed, but from it would come all sorts of future communication.

Bell and Watson also experimented with sounding devices, bull-horns, and other means of transmitting sound. They found the human voice to be the best of all, but the current was so weak that they usually had to shout to make themselves heard. Some of the first users of the system were put off by what they considered to be excessive noise.

continuing to pluck the reed when I was startled by a loud shout from Bell and out he rushed in great excitement to see what I was doing.[4]

Without attempting to, Watson had sent "a sound-shaped electric current"[5] from one room to another. Though quite a few inventors and scientists had attempted this, to our knowledge this was the first documented success.

Within a few days, Bell had invited Gardiner Greene Hubbard and Thomas Sanders to his rented rooms. Their ears were not as discriminating, and they did not see all the potential Bell did, but both men were heartened by the exhibitions. Just as he was starting to think of his protégé as a success, however, Gardiner Hubbard learned that he wanted to court his daughter.

ROMANCE

Coincidentally, Bell's scientific quest developed with his romantic one. We do not know how long it took from the first time he met Mabel Hubbard to fall in love, but we know he was head-over-heels in love with her by June 1875, the same month he heard that first twang on the telephone wire. Three weeks after his scientific success, Bell approached Mr. and Mrs. Hubbard to ask permission to court their daughter. Both parents were appalled, in part because they thought Bell was actually eight years older than he was. The Hubbards extracted a promise from Bell not to mention his interest to Mabel for a full calendar year. They apparently thought that settled the matter, but Bell, ever an impetuous man, could not keep the truth concealed for long.

First he endured a painful evening at the Hubbard house in Cambridge, unable to reveal his feelings. Then he wrote a long letter to Mabel, who had gone to Nantucket for summer vacation. Too impatient to wait, he brought the letter by hand, showing up at her door on the island where, for the first time, the 17-year-old learned of her tutor's feelings.

She did not return his feelings, at least not yet. She liked him, she said, but she did not love him. That was enough for Bell, who was then able to return to the waiting game. So, it was back to the inventor's workshop.

IMPROVEMENTS

Bell, it seemed, never had the luxury of working on one thing at a time. This was in part because of his temperament: He always accepted new challenges and took on new projects. It was also because his romantic quest was intertwined with his quest for invention. Now that he had revealed his interest in Mabel Hubbard, his relationship with Gardiner Greene Hubbard became more important than ever. It was quite apparent that the older man wanted to rein in the younger one. If only Bell would concentrate on one thing—the harmonic telegraph—he would make enough money so that one day he could marry Mabel, live comfortably, and be free to pursue his other interests. Gardiner Hubbard's words of advice sound practical and wise to us today, but had Bell heeded them entirely, he would not have invented the telephone. He would be a footnote in the history of science instead of a giant. Bell had fastened on to the telephone idea and he would not let go.

Bell was not the first to surmise the telephone concept. A German schoolteacher, Philip Reiss, was a pioneer of the transmission of voices a decade earlier, but he had never patented his work. Thomas Edison, who was the same age as Bell, was in the early stages of telephone development. Others, like Moses Farmer of Boston, the inventor of the first fire alarm, were peeking around the same corners. So, what did Bell bring that was so different?

First, he had an exquisite sense and understanding of sound (Edison, by contrast, was nearly deaf). Second, he was willing to experiment with all sorts of materials and reach many partial dead ends on the way to success. Third, he had the perfect assistant in Thomas Watson who, with notice of only a day or two, could put together almost any mechanical contraption Bell designed. The two men worked more closely than ever in the fall of 1875, and by the beginning of 1876, they had progressed far enough that Gardiner Greene Hubbard practically begged Bell to patent his invention.

ONE DAY; TWO PATENTS

With his deaf students, his lectures at Boston University, and his late-night experiments, Bell was so overextended that he did not file the patent himself in Washington, D.C. Instead, Gardiner Greene Hubbard, who saw the need for haste, found two attorneys to file the patent on his behalf. On February 14, 1876, just a bit shy of Bell's thirtieth birthday, his agents took his "Improvement in Telegraphy" to the U.S. Patent Office in Washington, D.C. By the oddest of coincidences, Elisha Gray, who had been Bell's competitor for some time, went to the patent office later on that same day to file a caveat, or a signal of intent to patent in the future. Bell's lawyers beat Elisha Gray to the patent office by about four hours that day, but the real patent decision would be made on the basis of priority of concept and design, rather than on the difference of four hours.

The patent officials examined both requests and saw no apparent conflict between them. Gray's request was for a caveat; he did not actually have a device ready to be tested. Bell had filed a request for an actual patent, and his extensive record-keeping made it clear that he had been working on his invention for more than two years. Even so, historians of the case have long pointed out that Bell had the assistance of an employee of the patent office who, illegally, showed Bell some of Gray's caveat application. Patent officials made their decision on March 3, 1878 (Bell's thirtieth birthday), and awarded the actual patent on March 7. Given that historians often call this the most valuable patent in American history, it is worth quoting some of the particulars.

FAC-SIMILE DU TÉLÉPHONE ORIGINAL D ALEXANDRE GRAHAM BELL
CONSTRUIT PAR LA WESTERN ELECTRIC Cᵒ
OFFERT PAR LA SOCIÉTÉ ANONYME "LE MATÉRIEL TÉLÉPHONIQUE"

This is a copy of the first telephone, patented by Bell in 1876. In his patent application, Bell wrote that his telephone used a "vibratory or undulatory current of electricity . . . and [an] apparatus for, producing electrical undulations upon the line wire . . . [such] that communication in both directions is established."

My present invention consists in the employment of a vibratory or undulatory current of electricity in contradistinction to a merely intermittent or pulsatory current, and of a method of, and apparatus for, producing electrical undulations upon the line wire. . . . The advantages I claim to derive from the use of an undulatory current in place of a merely intermittent one are, first, that a very much larger number of signals can be transmitted simultaneously on the same circuit; second, that a closed circuit and single main battery may be used; third, that communication in both directions is established."[6]

Bell did not mention voices or speech, and the word *telephone* never appeared. Even at this moment, when he had broken new ground in the history of technology, Bell still used the terminology of the past three decades: He spoke of telegraphy, messages, and the ability to transmit more than one message at once. The confusion between the discovery and the description of that discovery is somewhat like Christopher Columbus who, upon discovering the Americas in 1492, claimed to have reached the outlying areas of China and Japan.

FIRST WORDS

Bell was not in Washington to receive the patent; he was working hard in Boston. He and Mabel Hubbard were overjoyed to hear of its approval because they had overcome her parents' objections to become engaged toward the end of 1875, and the two were impatient for Bell to have enough worldly success for them to marry. Meanwhile, Bell and Watson moved on to what would be, both for them and for posterity, one of the great culminations of their work. Bell's scientific notebook tells us of the events of March 10, 1876:

Mr. Watson was stationed in one room with the receiving instrument. He pressed one ear closely against S [the instrument] and closed his other ear with his hand. The transmitting instrument was placed in another room and the doors of both rooms were closed.

I shouted into M [a mouthpiece] the following sentence: "Mr. Watson—Come here—I want to see you." To my delight he came and declared that he had heard and understood what I said.

I asked him to repeat the words—He answered "You said, 'Mr. Watson—come here—I want to see you.'" We then changed places and I listened at S while Watson read a few passages from a book into the mouthpiece. It was certainly the case that articulate sounds proceeded from S.[7]

Bell's description makes the event sound perfectly normal. His scientific notebook does not convey the tremendous excitement he must have felt, or the fact that he had done what no one else had ever done before: transmitted speech over a wire through use of electricity. Quite possibly, Bell remained calm and neutral in his notebook explanation precisely because he knew he might one day have to defend his statements in court. That would explain why he claimed that "articulate sounds proceeded from S," a more modest and defensible statement than if he had said "articulate *speech* proceeded from S."

Generations of Americans have been told that Bell said "Mr. Watson—come here—I want to see you" because he had spilled battery acid on his pants and needed help. This account comes from a later recollection of Thomas Watson, and Bell's scientific notebook neither confirms nor denies the possibility. What we can say, with some confidence, is that these were the first words ever transmitted by what we call a telephone today, although Bell still called it the harmonic telegraph. They were not the last.

Philadelphia

"I shall do just whatever your father thinks best—and stay just as long as he thinks advisable—if you will promise to have some *red* roses for me when I return."
—*Alexander Graham Bell to Mabel Hubbard*

June 25, 1876, is a red-letter date in American history. Most of us know it, appropriately, as the day of the Battle of the Little Big Horn, where Custer and his cavalry troopers perished. It was also the day the telephone, as opposed to the harmonic telegraph, made its first appearance to the world.

THE CENTENNIAL EXHIBITION

In the early part of June 1876, Alexander Graham Bell was in a terrible hurry, which was his usual state. He was still working to perfect the telephone, as he had started to call it; he was in the midst of grading student papers at Boston University; and he was still tutoring several clients in his private practice. In the midst of all his work, he received an urgent summons to Philadelphia.

Several years in the planning, the Centennial Exhibition of 1876 commemorated the nation's birthday: It was 100 years since Thomas Jefferson had penned the Declaration of Independence. Meant as more than just a commemoration, the Centennial Exhibition was intended to show off American know-how and ingenuity to the rest of the world. All of the most recent American inventions—including two enormous Corliss steam engines—were on view, and visitors could go to literally hundreds of exhibits on everything from the sewing machine to the typewriter, and perhaps even the telephone.

Gardiner Greene Hubbard was in Philadelphia to set up a booth and exhibit space for Bell, who was still back in Boston. Hubbard telegraphed his future son-in-law to come quickly, as the last week of June was when judges would visit each of the booths to award prizes. Feeling torn between the demands imposed by his teaching schedule and his inventions, Bell hesitated. Bell family tradition has it that Mabel Hubbard persuaded him, even to the point of pushing him onto the train in Boston. Whether that story is completely true cannot be known, but Bell wrote to her from New York City the next day:

> My darling May,
>
>   There is no turning back now! Here I am in New York and shall be in Philadelphia tonight. I have been dreaming of your poor dear pale face all night long—and feel quite guilty about it. You know my darling that I love you far better than my normal classes [at Boston University]—so I shall try to be patient in Philadelphia for your sake. Don't worry yourself about me—I shall do just whatever your father thinks best—and stay just as long as he thinks advisable—if you will promise to have some *red* roses for me when I return.[1]

Again, we see how Bell the romantic and Bell the inventor worked in tandem. If not for the need to make money so he could persuade his future father-in-law to allow the marriage, Bell might not have advertised the telephone at all!

Arriving in Philadelphia on June 19, Bell worked with Gardiner Greene Hubbard to set up the telephone exhibit. Bell's exhibition ticket, which still survives, shows a photograph of a rather pale, even nervous, young man (one is reminded of his description of Mabel's "poor dear pale face"), but the eyes show a purposeful intensity. All was ready by the morning of June 25, which, coincidentally, was the same dawn that saw Custer and his Seventh Cavalry approach the banks of the Little Big Horn in far-off Montana.

The day was stifling hot, and Bell and his assistants (one of whom was Willie Hubbard, Gardiner Greene Hubbard's nephew) grew weary as they waited for the judges to appear. June 25 had been scheduled as the day when the judges would circulate; for that reason, there was no public admittance that day, and the quiet was as oppressive as the heat.

Years later, in retelling the story, Bell often made it sound as if it was purely by chance that he received unexpected assistance, but today we know that he had met Dom Pedro, the emperor of Brazil, in Boston 11 days earlier when the emperor had visited the Boston School for Deaf Mutes. Bell had sent the emperor two textbooks, and when Dom Pedro and the judges came to his part of the exhibition, Bell was able to act as if he were on friendly terms with the most important foreign dignitary to visit the exhibition, when actually they were barely acquainted.

Even so, a nodding acquaintance would not have helped if Bell had not been prepared. Toward the end of that hot afternoon, he guided the emperor and the American judges to his booth to demonstrate the new "speaking" telephone. With the emperor was Sir William Thomson (later called Lord Kelvin), a very important British scientist. Sir William was the first person to use the receiver while Bell was out of the room. Upon hearing some strange sounds, he started, for Bell spoke to him, "Do you understand what I say?"[2] Amazed, Sir William put down the receiver and went to look for Bell. Next to pick up the receiver was Emperor Dom Pedro, who held it for a moment or two. His countenance changed dramatically as he said "I hear, I hear!"[3] Bell was at the other end of the line, quoting from Hamlet's famous soliloquy, "To be or not to be." Like Sir William, the emperor ran to find the inventor.

That same day, early in the evening, Elisha Gray came to Bell's hotel. The two men had a friendly conversation, in which Gray made no claim to have a stronger or prior form of telephone invention. The field seemed to be Bell's and his alone.

To say that Bell succeeded at the Centennial Exhibition is an understatement. In front of a foreign head of state and a knighted scientist, he demonstrated the success of the telephone. Alone, among the inventors of his time, he had transmitted articulate speech. The distance was only 500 feet (91.44 meters), but this in no way diminished his success.

What about George Armstrong Custer? The colonel and his men perished on the banks of the Little Big Horn that same day, but Americans did not learn of it until 12 days later, on July 7. The reasons for the delay were numerous. First, there were no survivors of Custer's cavalry group. Second, when fellow cavalry troopers learned the terrible news, they had to send a messenger on a very fast horse hundreds of miles to the nearest telegraph office to send a message to New York City. The editors of the major New York newspapers did not respond at once, partly because the news seemed so fantastic and partly because they did not wish to run an unconfirmed story. When the editors finally released the tale, on July 7, the American public was incensed, and they demanded revenge. Few people at the time appreciated that on the same day that Custer met his fate, a new invention was shown, one that could cut the delay in such messages from 12 days to a few hours.

One day—far in the future—the delay would be only a matter of minutes.

DEMONSTRATIONS

Although Bell did not know it, his life was about to change for good. The solitary inventor was about to turn into a man of affairs, as well as a married one.

As late as the end of 1876, Bell still referred to his instrument as a harmonic telegraph or to his inventions as improvements to telegraphy. By early 1877, however, he was using the word *telephone*. In January of that year, he received his second major patent for the magneto electric telephone, the transmitter of the human voice. The time had come to take his success to the general public.

So, soon after passing his thirtieth birthday in March 1877, Bell began a series of lectures in the greater Boston area. At first, he and Thomas Watson, who was still his chief assistant, were only two or three miles (3 or 4.8 kilometers) apart as they transmitted words and sometimes songs across the wires. As they began to extend the distance, they hit one of their biggest successes when Bell lectured in Salem and received messages from Watson in Boston: 20 miles (32 kilometers) away. This seems unremarkable to us today, but to those who observed this demonstration, and others that followed, it seemed little short of a miracle. The *Boston Advertiser* ran two columns on its front page, with the left one showing the words uttered by Bell and the right one displaying the echo-back, or return talk, of Watson. Hard though it was to believe, the era of the electrically conveyed, speaking telephone had begun.

New York City received a demonstration of its own in May 1877. The *New York Times* reported:

> At Chickering Hall last evening, before about 300 persons, Professor Alexander Graham Bell lectured on "Sound and Electricity," and gave an exhibition of the speaking telephone.... He then went into an exhaustive discussion of

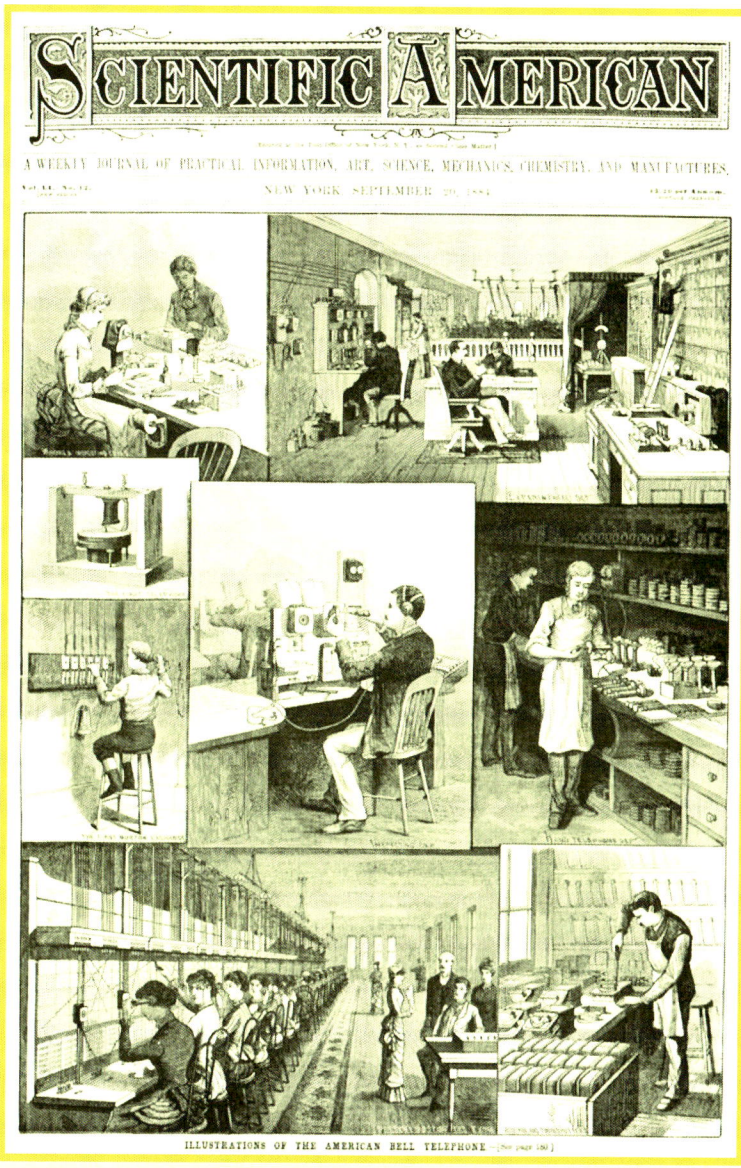

This page from *Scientific American* shows scenes from the Bell Company, as daily operations would have been carried out in 1884.

the transmission of sound by electricity and a history of the telephone, illustrated by a number of complex and not very intelligible figures cast upon, a prepared background.[4]

If this sounds as if the lecture was less than successful, consider what happened when Bell opened a large box and announced that he would speak to Thomas Watson in New Brunswick, New Jersey, 32 miles (51.5 kilometers) away:

> He thus telegraphed [newspapers were slow to catch on to "telephoned"] to New Brunswick, and shortly after, from a little box on the stage and from other instruments in different parts of the hall, came the music of the song known as "The sweet by and be." This was followed by "Home Sweet Home," and afterward by "Hold the Fort," sung by a strong baritone voice, and plainly audible. After this, Professor Bell and Mr. C.W. Field asked a number of questions through the telephone.[5]

Watson's was the strong baritone voice and Mr. C.W. Field was none other than Cyrus West Field, who had led the way in laying the first transatlantic cable. Perhaps not everyone was convinced—people continued to think there must be some sleight of hand in the telephone business—but to share the stage with Cyrus West Field meant that Alexander Graham Bell had come a very long way indeed.

INCORPORATION

By the early summer of 1877, Bell and Watson, as well as their financial backers Hubbard and Sanders, were persuaded they sat on a pile of gold. The telephone would make them all rich, if only they could establish incontrovertible proof that it belonged to them. Toward that end they formed the first telephone company on July 9, 1877.

The Bell Company superseded an earlier set of oral agreements between the four men. Given that Thomas Watson played such an important part in both the creation and the demonstration of the invention, Bell and his financial backers cut Watson in with an agreement to split company shares at 30–30–30–10 percent. Bell, Hubbard, and Sanders would each get 30 percent shares, and Watson would get 10 percent. Small as this sounds, it had the possibility to make millionaires out of all of them. Just two days later, Bell fulfilled his fondest hope and dream by marrying Mabel Hubbard. In an extremely chivalrous—some might say reckless—gesture, he handed all but 10 of his Bell Company shares to her as a wedding gift.

TRIP OF A LIFETIME

Just weeks after their wedding, the Bells embarked for England. Seven years had passed since Bell had seen his homeland, and he had to be conscious of the fact that he had departed it as practically unknown and was to return as a conquering hero. True, the British public was not as excited about the telephone as Americans were, but Bell was about to become famous on both sides of the Atlantic.

It is hard to say why the telephone was less embraced by Britons than Americans, but it was a pattern that would hold true for other European nations, including France, Germany, and Spain. Perhaps it was because Europeans lived closer to each other than Americans did, but Englishmen, Frenchmen, and Germans seemed much less likely to leap to buy a telephone. To many of them, the telegraph seemed the epitome of technological achievement, and the new telephone seemed like no more than a toy. Generally speaking, it was Europeans who looked at things this way, but Americans sometimes had similar thoughts.

The Bells settled happily in London. A.G. Bell delighted in renewing old friendships and acquaintances, and his wife took equal pleasure in creating new ones; despite her deafness, Mabel Bell was much more sociable than her inventor husband. Bell tried his hand at promoting the telephone, with only modest success, but he had an extraordinary moment on January 14, 1878, when he was allowed to demonstrate it to Queen Victoria, the same monarch who had sent the first transatlantic telegram 20 years earlier. "Most extraordinary" was all the Queen would say.

Almost a year in England ended with the Bells returning first to Canada and then to the United States. One of the first letters they received, upon arrival, was from Thomas Watson who, with typical wit, imitated Bell's famous first words, "Mr. Bell," he wrote, "Come here—I want to see you." So did many other telephone inventors, enthusiasts, and imitators. The race to see who would obtain the profits had heated up considerably.

Courtrooms and Boardrooms

"If Bell had been in Boston I should have invited him to join in one of our old war dances."

—*Thomas A. Watson*

Alexander Graham Bell knew he was an inventor, not a man of business. In a letter to his new father-in-law, Bell confessed that he dreaded being locked up in boardrooms rather than inventing rooms. Gardiner Greene Hubbard knew his son-in-law quite well, so he agreed that Bell should remain at the forefront of the inventing process, and Hubbard should be the telephone's chief promoter.

FIRST MOVES OUTWARD

The year that Bell and his wife spent in England (1877–1878) was a pivotal one as far as the fortunes of the Bell Company were concerned. Although the inventor was away, the promoter, financial backer, and chief engineer were on the scene, and they pursued their work with vigor.

Gardiner Greene Hubbard was an excellent promoter. Many years spent as an attorney and as a man-about-town

THOMAS A. EDISON
(1847–1931)

American Inventor

Born a few weeks apart in the late winter of 1847, Thomas Alva Edison and Alexander Graham Bell could hardly have been more different. They did share, however, an indomitable perseverance in the pursuit of invention.

Thomas Edison was born in Milan, Ohio. His father was a shingle maker and his mother was a schoolteacher. Thomas's parents moved from Canada during a political disturbance in 1838, and he grew up midway between Cleveland and Detroit. Adroit and entrepreneurial from his earliest days, Edison sold vegetable produce, newspapers, and candy, both to neighbors and then to passengers on the nearby railroad line. Like many American boys of that time, he was eager, alert, and industrious, but he also possessed a singular belief that what he dreamed could come to pass. This was what he and Bell shared.

Starting his career as a telegrapher, Edison showed great aptitude for all sorts of mechanical devices, even though his hearing began to deteriorate while he was still a teenager. Moving to Boston in 1868, he worked for Western Union Telegraph Company and conducted experiments in the Charles Williams Electrical Shop—the same one where Alexander Graham Bell and Thomas Watson would meet a few years later. By the early 1870s, Edison was working on his own version of what was called the harmonic telegraph; he in Washington, D.C. had made him familiar with both the process and the style needed to sell the telephone. Hubbard undertook a number of trips around the East Coast, talking up the telephone and persuading some businesses to adopt it. Hubbard was also the person responsible for the idea of leasing

eventually patented the quadraplex telegraph, which allowed four messages to be sent and received at the same time.

Edison and Bell first came in contact, and conflict, in the late 1870s. Believing that it could beat Bell's patents in court, Western Union hired Edison to improve on Bell's telephone. In a remarkably short time, Edison designed and patented the carbon-button transmitter, far superior to what Bell had patented in 1877. The two inventors appeared on a collision course, but this was prevented by a legal settlement under which the Bell Company was able to absorb Edison's patent. The carbon-button was used for many years afterwards.

As is the case with many great inventors, Edison had to spend almost as much time and money to defend his patents as to create new inventions. Unlike Bell, who soon wearied of legal battles, Edison accepted them as a sort of challenge: He once fought Western Union and the financier Jay Gould for years, to be awarded one dollar in damages!

Edison outlived Bell by seven years. By the time he died, the grand period of individual inventing had come to an end, replaced by the more systematic, large-scale inventing done in company laboratories. As someone who had been there at the lonely and inspired beginning, Edison had the privilege of seeing the whole process change. He is said to have declared that genius was "two percent inspiration and 98 percent perspiration."

telephones rather than selling them. His experience in other businesses persuaded him that the Bell Company needed to keep control of its instruments; therefore, it began and maintained the policy that telephones could be rented by agents in different cities who would then lease them to individuals or businesses. The leasing policy became a staple of the Bell Company, something which lasted long after Hubbard had departed the scene.

No one could question Hubbard's salesmanship skill or his vigor. Although he was in his late fifties, he promoted the telephone more effectively than many a younger man might have done. He was, like his son-in-law, inclined to slapdash methods when it came to business. No one could better present the product and close a sale or a lease, but Hubbard was poor at record-keeping, and he made many spontaneous arrangements and agreements with agents, leading to a multiplicity of contracts. In just the one year that Bell was in England, the Bell Company simultaneously expanded and lost track of its mission.

Hubbard naturally denied this, but Thomas Sanders, who was providing the money to keep the company afloat, saw how dangerous the situation was. Although he admired Hubbard's energy and nerve, he nonetheless fretted over the state of the company's finances, and Sanders eventually plowed $110,000 (about five times more than the lifetime wages of an average laborer during this era) of his own money into the Bell Company before getting anything back.

Thomas Watson, meanwhile, was the chief engineer and technical man in Bell's absence. Nothing if not energetic, Watson worked on a new double-coiled ringer, which would eventually lead to the possibility of party lines, with two or more persons sharing the same telephone line. Watson was also the first to see the danger in the competition from Thomas Edison, who had just devised a carbon receiver on behalf of Western Union.

LEGAL CHALLENGES

The greatest danger came from the Western Union Telegraph Company, which was perhaps the largest and most profitable American business firm of the 1870s. Sometime in 1877—the exact date is uncertain—Bell and his father-in-law actually offered their entire new enterprise to Western Union for $100,000. Although that six-figure amount would have meant a lot to Bell and Hubbard at the time, it was a paltry figure compared with what the Bell Company would be worth in the future. The Western Union Company turned the offer down, probably because its leaders believed they controlled the industry. Why spend money on a new-fangled thing that had yet to show it would make a profit? In hindsight, this has to be seen as one of the single worst business decisions of the entire nineteenth century.

Just months later, sometime in 1878, Western Union realized its mistake. As the use of the telephone began to spread—thanks to the promotion of Gardiner Greene Hubbard—Western Union sponsored a team of inventors, including Elisha Gray, Thomas Dolbear, and Thomas Edison. Given Western Union's great financial resources, there was every reason to believe that the giant would strangle the baby in its crib.

Gardiner Greene Hubbard had been a foe of Western Union for many years. As a patent attorney and adviser to Congress, he had long urged that Western Union's grip on communications be loosened, or at least that the company be required to acknowledge its obligation to serve the public. Now Hubbard had a weapon to use against his old foe, and some would claim he used it like a cudgel.

The biggest problem was Western Union's ubiquitous presence. The great telegraph company had poles and wires strung around most of the country, while the tiny Bell Company had only a handful. In the early days of telephone use, each person who leased a Bell Company phone had to have a separate line directed to each person to whom he talked. This meant a great

This photograph of Thomas Edison and his phonograph was taken between 1870 and 1880. Today, Edison is considered one of the most prolific inventors in American history—with more than 1,000 patents in his name.

multiplicity of lines, wires, and poles. Western Union could, and did, deny the Bell Company access to its own lines, leading to further confusion and trouble. This seemed like a David-versus-Goliath contest, with the Bell Company doomed from the start.

But David had a stone, and the Bell Company had the patents of 1876 and 1877. In the first patent, Bell had outlined his improvements to telegraphy, especially the importance of the concept of variable resistance, which he called the intermittent current. In the second patent, he had shown how his magneto electric telephone could be used. Gardiner Greene Hubbard, a patent lawyer by training, saw these two pieces of authenticated paper as the legal basis for the Bell Company's existence, and he brought suit for patent infringement against the Western Union Telegraph Company in 1879.

THE *DOWD* CASE

Bell was naturally summoned, time and again, as the chief witness for the Bell Company. By nature he was disinclined to this sort of legal contest, but by academic training he was well suited for it. Gardiner Greene Hubbard had advised him, even before he married his daughter, to save all sorts of documents that could prove his case, and Bell also had a remarkable memory. The result was that the Bell Company had a chief witness who could stay on the stand as long as six hours at a time (it happened once or twice), answering all sorts of questions that required both technical skill and good memory to answer. Time and again, Bell proved equal to the challenge; yet victory was by no means assured.

The most serious challenge to Bell the inventor and to the Bell Company was the charge that Bell had stolen the concept of variable resistance. Bell had plenty of notes about other parts of his inventive process, but the notion of variable resistance had developed along the way, and he had no special way to verify it. His legal opponents pointed out that in his second patent, of January 1877, his notations on variable resistance had been attached to a piece of paper and were clearly written in a handwriting that was different from the rest of the pages. This was because Bell had hired a copyist or secretary. Elisha Gray, now chief engineer for Western Union, claimed Bell had stolen the idea.

How could he have stolen the idea? Gray claimed Bell had bribed a patent office employee with $100, and that this employee had then allowed Bell to examine Gray's caveat, which was the first stage toward an actual patent, sometime in 1876. The patent office employee did not confirm the statement during the case of 1879, but he made a deposition in 1885 that verified most of Gray's story.

Historians of technology have argued, and will continue to argue, the point. Was Bell the sole inventor of the telephone, or did he piggy-back on the ideas of Elisha Gray? We will save our final words on this for Chapter 10.

As it turned out, the chief attorney for Western Union became convinced that his case was a lost cause. The more Bell sat in the witness box, the more convincing his explanations became, and the more the evidence favored the Bell Company. In the autumn of 1879, this attorney urged his superiors at Western Union to give up the fight, and on November 10, a historic agreement was reached in an out-of-court settlement. Under its provisions:

Western Union would stick to telegraphy and stay out of the telephone business;

The Bell Company would be free to use Thomas Edison's carbon transmitter;

The Bell Company would be able to use Western Union's telegraph lines; and

Western Union would receive a 20 percent share of the net profits of the Bell Company for 14 years, the period of which Bell's patents ran.

Thomas Watson later described his reaction to the news of victory in the *Dowd* case: "If Bell had been in Boston I should have invited him to join in one of our old war dances but, as he was not available, I had to have the dance all to myself, celebrating this great event in my life with a whole day alone in my old haunts—the woods and shores of Swampscott and Marblehead, declaiming to the skies all the poetry I remembered."[1]

There is no doubt that this was a personal triumph for Alexander Graham Bell, but it was an even greater triumph for the Bell Company, which would have the field to itself for the next 14 years. It is at this point that the tale of Alexander Graham Bell begins to separate from that of the Bell Company, and indeed from the telephone itself. The inventor was weary from having to defend his actions in court. He wanted to be free to pursue other interests. Meanwhile, the Bell Company slipped right out from the hands of his father-in-law.

PARTING WAYS

Until 1880, the Bell Company was run pretty much as a family-and-friends enterprise. Bell was the designing genius; his father-in-law Hubbard was the skillful promoter; Thomas Watson was the maker and implanter of materials; and Thomas Sanders provided the capital. By 1880, however, it was apparent that this close group of friends and in-laws was unable to cope with the demands presented by moving from a small organization to a large one.

Bell was the first, and the happiest, to leave. When the Bell Company reorganized its board of directors in 1880, he asked to be left off, and by 1881, he had left the company entirely.

Gardiner Greene Hubbard put up the sternest fight. Convinced that the Bell Company was the product of his son-in-law's genius and his own devotion, he tried but failed to keep the reins within the Bell-Hubbard family.

Thomas Sanders was about neutral, so far as the end was concerned. He had put up most of his personal fortune to get the Bell Company off the ground; what he now wanted was to secure a good return on his investment.

Thomas Watson stayed on the longest, until about 1882, but the fun went out of it. He had always thrived while he worked in tandem with Bell, and Watson left the company with no regrets.

By the beginning of the 1880s, the board of directors and governorship of the Bell Company had thoroughly changed. William Hathaway Forbes, a Boston Brahmin, had become the first president of the new American Bell Telephone Company. Born into a family of means, Forbes had a shaky beginning in life: He had been expelled from Harvard, but he had rebuilt his reputation as a dashing Civil War cavalryman, and he had also married a daughter of Ralph Waldo Emerson. Forbes now brought his vigor and spirit to the American Bell Company.

Chauncey Smith, another Bostonian, was the chief legal counsel for the company. A man of great height, bulk, and friendliness, he appeared to be like the "Vicar of Wakefield," but anyone who met him in court was more likely to compare him with Napoleon or George Armstrong Custer. Smith became the chief defender of the Bell patents.

James J. Storrow, also a Bostonian, was another prominent attorney who served the Bell Company. Hailing from the family for which the famous Storrow Drive is named, he was a shrewd judge of patents, contests, and of public opinion (in this he was far in advance of his fellows).

The new group of company leaders took over where Bell, Hubbard, Sanders, and Watson had left. None of the new group had the genius of Bell or the promoting spirit of Hubbard, but they shared a vision: to keep the Bell Company number one in the telephone business.

Social and Economic Change

"[May we all] be gathered together in a heaven of ever-lasting rest and peace and bliss—except the inventor of the telephone."

—*Mark Twain, 1890*

As far as the public was concerned, the telephone first appeared in the 1880s. By no small coincidence, that was also the decade that saw the advent of electric lights and underground subway tunnels. Urban Americans who lived in cities of 100,000 or more saw their lives change dramatically during the 1880s. Rural Americans, especially those who lived in towns of 5,000 or fewer, took longer to see the technological changes that were under way.

LINES AND WIRES

The cities were electrified first, and they also received the first telephone service. The Bell Company, assured of a virtual monopoly until 1893, moved quickly to establish service in Boston and New York.

In the beginning, each telephone required a separate line, wired to the exact house with which communication was desired. This led to a frightful number of overhead wires, as well as telephone poles that seemed ready to block out the sunlight. There were no switchboards—at least not right away—and Bell Company customers often experienced frustration as they tried to establish connections. "Hello! Are you there? Is this a secure line?" was frequently heard.

From Hartford, Connecticut, came one of the loudest yelps of all. Mark Twain, the great American humorist, had been born and raised in Missouri, but he now lived in Hartford. Twain thought that the telephone would aid him in his writing, especially because he could phone local newspaper editors, and he had one of the first telephones in his area. By 1890, he had become so discouraged that he wrote a letter to the New York *World*: "It is my heart-warm and world-embracing Christmas hope and aspiration that all of us—the high, the low, the rich, the poor, the admired, the despised, the loved, the hated, the civilized, the savage—may eventually be gathered together in a heaven of everlasting rest and peace and bliss—except the inventor of the telephone."[1]

Gardiner Greene Hubbard, who had long been out of the business, wrote Twain in good humor, asking what he meant. Addressing his letter to the "Father-in-Law of the Telephone," Twain replied that his seldom worked properly. One practically had to shout into it to be heard, and when a connection was finally established, the rude and impertinent operators would often cut a conversation off in mid-sentence.

Accustomed as we are to excellent telephone service, it is difficult to know just how many dilemmas the early Telephone

The General Services Administration telephone switchboard and its operators, which at the time handled calls going to 20,000 government phones, are seen during a busy afternoon in August 1951. Switchboards were a common way of managing telephone lines well into the twentieth century.

Pioneers (an official organization of telephone service operators) faced. It was natural that the Bell Company would make its first significant attempts in Boston and New York, but it

THE BLIZZARD OF '88

Americans of the nineteenth century were as keenly interested in the weather as we are today. Global warming did not seem a big threat at the time; indeed, many people spoke of global cooling.

The winter of 1888 was fairly mild through January and February, with few complaints from New Englanders or New Yorkers. Then there came one of the biggest of all winter storms on March 11 and 12, immortalized ever since as the "Blizzard of '88."

Snow and ice fell, fell, and continued to fall. Most New Yorkers were content to stay inside for a day or two, but they were appalled to see most of their services disappear (above ground water mains and gas lines quickly froze). First the electric light failed, then the elevated trains did the same, and finally telephone service virtually ceased.

If there was one service New Yorkers expected to hold up in such a storm, it was the telephone, and today it probably would do so. Almost all of New York's telephone wires were outside and above ground, and the winds and snow conspired to topple most of the heavily laden poles in Manhattan. The biggest of all, near Wall Street, toppled over, creating a terrific mess. Other poles caved in the roofs of buildings.

When the storm finally abated, New Yorkers turned their attention to the future. The biggest change was that telephone lines would be laid underground. This massive undertaking began in the summer of 1888 and was substantially finished within two years. Almost from that point forward, the placement of telephone lines became a matter of social standing, as well as utility. Wealthy East Coast Americans in places like Newport, New York, and Bar Harbor insisted that their lines be placed underground, while plebian Americans, especially in rural areas, continued to have obvious lines, wires, and figure patterns in the sky.

was also natural that it would run into all sorts of difficulties. Cities often lacked municipal planners in those days, and the first poles and wires were often strung up regardless of passing traffic or natural obstructions. Subscribers to the new telephone service naturally wanted perfect tonal quality, but the very ground under their feet was changing, due to the creation of subway tunnels. The first telephone circuits were one-way and wired to the ground, and early telephone conversations picked up all sorts of static.

Then there was the issue of telephone etiquette. From the very beginning, Bell had expressed his belief that people calling each other should use nautical terminology, as in "Hoy, hoy!" This led to many early conversations that began with "Hoy, Watson!" and "Hoy, Bell!"[2] Thomas Edison, whose carbon transmitter had been appropriated by the Bell Company, gained some measure of revenge: Americans much preferred his simple approach of "Hello." Within a few years, Edison's greeting supplanted Bell's.

There were other concerns, however. Who should initiate the conversation? Who should end the call? Should one properly identify oneself at the start of a call, or should one just ask for the person he or she wanted to reach? These questions were debated throughout the end of the nineteenth century, and they were only resolved by the publication of Emily Post's *Etiquette* in 1922.

Post did not dedicate any of the 38 chapters of her book to the telephone. Born in 1879, she clearly considered it something new, and perhaps less important than handwritten notes, of which she was an earnest admirer. She did, however, include some words of advice on telephone use in the chapter about invitations to breakfast, lunch, or tea. Here is the standard form that she recommended: "Is this Lenox 0000? Will you please ask Mr. and Mrs. Smith if they will dine with Mrs. Grantham Jones next Tuesday the tenth at eight o'clock? Mrs. Jones's telephone number is Plaza, one two ring two."[3]

The standard reply, given by Miss Post, was: "Mr. and Mrs. Huntington Smith regret that they will be unavailable to dine with Mrs. Jones on Tuesday the tenth as they are engaged for that evening."[4]

It is obvious that Emily Post believed that her readers had butlers or parlor maids who would convey these messages, which would make it unnecessary for the actual inviters or invitees to do the work. In the case of young children in the house, however, Miss Post recommended that the parents prepare a set of cards, with most of the formal language contained, so that they could simply fill in "Mr. and Mrs. Smith" or "Mrs. Jones" when they took a message.

Post's belief, echoed by many columnists since, was that a telephone was placed in a home for the convenience of the owner, not for those who wished to reach the home. Therefore, the person who called a private residence should identify himself or herself and courteously ask for the person to whom he or she wished to speak. Any wisecracking or attempt at humor was clearly out of bounds.

ON THE SWITCHBOARD

The switchboard was first invented by an undertaker, who was said to have been exasperated by local operators who, he believed, were diverting business away from him. He therefore designed an instrument by which all incoming calls could be routed to the numbers and extensions of other homes, making the multiplicity of wires unnecessary. This did not catch on in rural areas for a while, and the skyline of places like Wichita, Kansas, remained decorated with phone wires; but for most towns of 10,000 population, switchboards became routine. This created the question: What kind of person should run the switchboard?

At first it was believed that boys or young men would take these jobs. American boys spent much more time fiddling with gadgets than American girls did, and it seemed natural that boys would be better at handling the wires and finding the right sockets to plug them into. This era of the boy telephone operator proved short-lived indeed. The early telephone boys were surly, even rude, and it was impossible to keep them in one place to do their tasks. Within a few short years, girls or young women replaced boys throughout the Bell system, and the courteous, smooth voice of the female operator became nearly ubiquitous. Boys might know more about electricity and technology, but they could not be made to sit, listen, wait, and reply—all while maintaining perfectly good manners!

In 1885, the Bell Company created a wholly owned subsidiary named American Telephone and Telegraph (AT&T). Located in Manhattan, not Boston, this new company was intended solely for the transmission of long-distance calls; for some time it was called the "Long Distance Company." The creation of AT&T lent an even greater need for a standardized form of telephone courtesy, and young women soon went to finishing schools where they learned to modulate their voices to respond to all the customers' needs and never to bat an eyelash in the process.

TRAINS ON TIME

Time was not standardized until 1883. Until that year, there was no differentiation between Eastern, Central, Mountain, or Pacific times in the United States. One can argue there was no need for such differentiation, because the entire time distance in the United States is never more than four hours, and in the days of carriages, horses, and walking, one never needed to correct one's watch. The building of railroads, the creation of the telegraph, and finally the intrusion of the telephone all made time differentiation necessary, if only to ensure that train schedules were accurate.

Many of us today think of the telephone primarily as a social instrument, and the phone has certainly played an important part in our social lives. When it was pioneered in the last two decades of the nineteenth century, however, the telephone was seen primarily as a tool for business, and it has remained so ever since. This chapter is concerned both with the development of AT&T and the Bell companies and with the growth and change in American business as a whole during the early telephone era.

MONOPOLY ENDS

Alexander Graham Bell's two major patents—those of March 1876 and January 1877—expired in 1893 and 1894. The Bell companies, which then included New England Telephone, Bell Telephone, and AT&T, had enjoyed 14 years of monopoly, but it all came to an end in the last decade of the nineteenth century.

It is safe to say that monopoly had not been good, either for the Bell companies or for the general public. The Bostonian financial men who had run the Bell companies since Bell and his father-in-law bowed out were mostly interested in profits. They ran a tight business and did not care about improving or expanding service. The result was that people considered the Bell companies to be an oppressive and obnoxious monopoly. Most Americans were delighted to hear that the original patents had expired, which would open the way for general competition.

ERA OF THE INDEPENDENTS

Independent telephone companies soon sprang up in every city, county, and state. True, the industrial Northeast was hard to win over from the Bell system. Businessmen in New England and New York were so accustomed to Bell service that they scorned the independents. One's choice of service from either Bell or an independent company soon became yet another matter of social distinction, with old money tending toward the Bell companies. Newer regions of the country, where there were fewer rich and well-to-do, were more likely to embrace the independents, which had names like Kansas Telephone, Ohio Telephone, and the like. By about 1905, Iowa had a greater telephone-to-population ratio than any other state in the nation.

Indeed, the creation of new, independent companies was a boon for many rural Americans. The Bell companies had refused to expand service to many rural areas because they thought it would be unprofitable. Small new firms were more likely to seek out just those areas and to create the first exchanges and switchboards within them. By about 1905, independents gained almost a 50 percent share of the total market, and many rural Americans had telephones or access to one at a neighbor's home. The change cannot be overestimated; what had been unbearable conditions for a farmer's wife, in terms of loneliness, now became quite bearable.

Financially speaking, there was room for both the Bell companies and the independents, but Bell executives did not see things in this light. To most of them, the pre-1893 period seemed like a golden age, one in which they had done what they wanted as they wanted. Now they faced stiff competition, as well as the possibility of state regulation. Things might have continued in this direction were it not for the intervention of Wall Street bankers.

John Pierpont Morgan (whom everyone called "J.P.") was the richest, perhaps the most powerful, man in America. Born in the industrial Northeast, he had added to his father's success in banking through a series of mergers and consolidations. Today we would call him a robber baron (and many people of his time did so), but Morgan thought of himself in much more dignified terms. Like John D. Rockefeller, who had organized the Standard Oil Company, Morgan thought he performed a public service in his work. The public, he declared, was much better served by well-run conglomerates than by mom-and-pop stores. Only large companies, with access to capital, could undertake the kind of improvements needed to serve a truly national market.

THEODORE NEWTON VAIL
(1845–1920)

President of AT&T

Men of great influence seldom endear themselves to the average person; one thinks of Vanderbilt's famous saying "The public be damned!" There was something different about Theodore Vail. Even when he pursued what we might call predatory policies against his business competition, Vail seemed to act in what he perceived to be the public good.

His life was intermixed with communications from the start. Alfred Vail, his first cousin once removed, had been the personal assistant to Samuel F.B. Morse during the making of the telegraph. (One might say that Alfred Vail and Morse were akin to Thomas Watson and Alexander Graham Bell.) Born in New Jersey, Theodore Vail moved west with his family as an adolescent. He learned telegraphy in Iowa, then moved farther west to work for the Railway Mail Service; he eventually became general superintendent in 1876, the highest position attainable in the postal branch of the U.S. government. Gardiner Greene Hubbard hired him in 1878, and he soon became general manager of the Bell Telephone Company, and later of AT&T.

The very things that endeared Vail to midwesterners—his blunt, but friendly, manner and his method of acting in the public good—made him unpopular with Boston Brahmins. The Boston financiers

The debate about consolidation versus competition began in Morgan's time and continues into our own. Not even the best business historian has been able to set the matter completely straight. Is regulation or free enterprise, monopoly or competition, better for the consumer? One can say, quite clearly, that

who took over the Bell companies in 1880 slowly forced Vail out, and he retired to life on a grand scale, entertaining at his beloved Vermont estate, Speedwell Farms. Vail also dabbled in international investments, most of which did not pan out. He always claimed to be second-rate when it came to finance, and first-rate when it came to management and organization.

When AT&T asked him to come back, in the spring of 1907, Vail at first protested that he was too old for the job, but this was a polite cover. People at AT&T knew he was incredibly eager to resume what had long been his passion: the creation of universal service through one telephone company. Once back in the president's chair, Vail set a new standard for energy and organization; he wanted AT&T to absorb all its competitors and become one great, universal company.

Although he never attained the great goal of universality, Vail was one of the most successful and well-liked of all business executives. Government officials admired him, fellow businessmen feared him, and the general public thought better of him than of almost any other executive. It was partly a matter of his skill at public relations (Vail was one of the first executives to create a public relations department), but it also was a result of his personal style. Born in the East, matured in the West, he was more of an "all-around American" than Carnegie, Rockefeller, or the like.

people on both sides of the argument felt as passionately then as they do today.

Early in 1907, Morgan directed his attention to the telephone market. He had long observed the Bell companies from afar, and, from his point of view, they were the natural foundation of what might become a well-regulated monopoly. Most of the independents, by contrast, had very little capital, making them unappealing to Morgan and his banker friends. Through a series of moves, some surreptitious and others above board, Morgan gained a strong interest in Bell Company stock. Pressuring the boards of directors, he brought about a major change in May of that year when he brought in Theodore N. Vail as the new president of AT&T.

As discussed, in Chapter 8, Vail had been forced out of the telephone business. The syndicate of Boston businessmen who ran the show found him brash, cocky, and, above all, too public-minded. Vail had the temerity to suggest that profits did not always have to come first in the telephone business. Twenty years had passed since then, and though Vail spent time at his beloved Vermont estate and made business forays overseas, he had never lost his interest in telephones. At 62, he agreed to return.

VAIL'S POLICIES

Years had passed and the vigorous man of 30 had turned into the graybeard of 60. On first meeting Theodore Vail, many people thought him too kind, gentle, and even soft for such an important managerial role. They were mistaken, for beneath that kind exterior was one of the most relentless captains of industry ever seen on American soil.

Immediately upon becoming president of AT&T, Vail heeded the instructions of J.P. Morgan, who warned that the company must cut all sorts of expense and avoid many new ones. This went against Vail's nature, as he was naturally expansive and optimistic, but he went along with the New

York bankers and implemented a new austerity program. More important, his series of policy papers and speeches made him about the most visible captain of industry of his day. John D. Rockefeller might stay at home behind iron gates, and Andrew Carnegie might escape to Scotland, but Theodore N. Vail was very much on the scene, day after day.

Over the next 10 years, Vail put out a number of policy statements, which made him seem different from other industrial leaders. In one of the first, given in March 1908, he extolled the virtues of what the Bell system had to offer: "The strength of the Bell system lies in this 'universality.' It affords facilities to the public beyond those possible on any other lines. It carries with it also the obligation to occupy and develop the whole field. The urban field was the first to receive attention and the development keeps pace with the demand. The semi-urban and rural demand came later."[5]

Within months of assuming the presidency, Vail embarked on what had long been his fondest hope: to create a universal telephone service from coast to coast. As a young telegrapher he had seen the potential of mass communication; as an old executive, he now strove to make that potential a reality. To reach that goal, however, meant both sacrifice and aggression.

Vail faced the painful fact that the independent telephone companies controlled almost half of the market. He went on the offense, buying up as many as he could and denying connection of Bell Company lines to the rest. There were plenty of independent telephone companies ready for a fight, and Vail did not always win, but by the time Woodrow Wilson became the twenty-ninth president of the United States in 1913, the Bell companies were ascending.

Born in Virginia and educated at Johns Hopkins University, Wilson was one of the few true intellectuals to reach the White House. Although Wilson supported the ideas of the

AMERICAN TELEPHONE & TELEGRAPH COMPANY

SPECIAL V-88159

AMERICAN BANK NOTE COMPANY.

This is an early advertisement for the company American Telephone & Telegraph, more popularly known as AT&T. AT&T was a subsidiary of Bell's original company, Bell Telephone Company.

Progressive Movement, including ridding the nation of economic monopolies, he proved less dangerous to major corporations than their executives feared. For his part, Theodore Vail knew that AT&T, which had become the parent company of the entire Bell system, would have to compromise, even yield to some cherished desires, in order to survive the political storm that Wilson's election created. In November 1913, just eight months after Wilson's inauguration, AT&T pledged itself to the Kingsbury Commitment, named for the vice president of AT&T. In brief, AT&T agreed

To cease its practice of buying up independent
    telephone companies;

To divest itself of its majority stock holding in Western
    Electric; and

To allow any independent telephone company that
    wished to connect its lines to Bell Company lines
    to do so.

These seemed like extraordinary giveaways by Vail and
the Bell system, but they were necessary and Vail was wise
enough to know it. President Wilson hailed the Kingsbury
Commitment as a wise act, and the federal government fore-
stalled any action by its justice department against AT&T. Once
again, Vail had proved to be the indispensable man.

HELLO FRISCO, HELLO

Early in 1914, just before the outbreak of World War I, Vail
pledged that AT&T would fulfill its long-standing goal of establishing coast-to-coast telephone service. Many obstacles stood
in the way, including the Rocky Mountains, but the Bell system
had a number of new inventions to smooth the way, including
the vacuum tube, a device that improved signal transmissions.
There was still an enormous amount of work to do, including stringing poles and wires across the continent, but by the
last day of 1914, the job was complete. (By then, Europe was
embroiled in World War I.) Vail scheduled the magic moment
to unveil the service for January 25, 1915.

Vail asked Alexander Graham Bell to come out of retirement. Thomas Watson, also called from retirement, joined
the party, and in the afternoon of January 25, a large group of
distinguished-looking men gathered, half of them in New York
City and the others in San Francisco. Bell, who was 68 years old
at the time, was handed a replica of one of his earliest phones
and asked to speak into it: "Hello, Mr. Watson. Can you hear
me?" "I hear you perfectly," was the reply.[6]

AT&T company executives had been unsure how these two old compatriots would respond to some of the new technologies, but Bell and Watson seemed right at home. They spoke for about 23 minutes, and toward the end, Bell repeated his famous words from 1876: "Mr. Watson—come here—I want to see you."[7] Watson replied, somewhat sorrowfully, that he would be glad to oblige but it would take a full week to do so. He and Bell no longer worked in adjoining rooms; at that moment, they were separated by 3,000 miles (4,828 kilometers) of American landscape.

Theodore Vail was not on hand for the ceremony. A leg injury kept him at Jekyll Island, South Carolina, but he was able to listen to the famed conversation through the miracle of long-distance service. President Wilson, in Washington, was able to phone in to congratulate both Alexander Graham Bell and Theodore Vail. All told, it was a historic moment, one commemorated in the song "Hello Frisco, Hello."

WORLD WAR

World War I began in August 1914, just a few short months before the opening of the transcontinental telephone line. Americans were eager to be neutral in the Great War, as it was then called, but a set of circumstances—including the sinking of passenger ships—brought the United States into the war in 1917. Theodore Vail commented on the situation, in an essay published in *Agricultural Digest*: "We are in this war. We are in it to stay. The sooner we become effective, the more help we can give, the less we will have to do, and the sooner it will be over. The more dilatory we are, the greater burden we shall have to bear."[8]

This was spoken like a true exemplar of efficiency. Vail may have been surprised, however, by the demand and the burden that was put upon AT&T one year later. In the summer of 1918, President Wilson signed an executive order to nationalize AT&T, after advisers persuaded him that the war effort required government control of all communications. The great phone company was suddenly the property of the U.S. government.

Vail promptly moved the company out of its New York City headquarters, but few other changes were apparent. The federal government had neither the knowledge nor the expertise to run AT&T on its own, and most managers and employees remained in their positions. For his part, Vail won the admiration of the U.S. postmaster general, who was responsible for absorbing the phone company. Vail cooperated so fully that the postmaster general recommended a return to the old system as soon as possible, and by the early part of 1919, AT&T was back in private hands. The government's attempt to nationalize AT&T showed the importance of telephone communications, something that would only increase in the years to come.

The Man,
the Invention,
the Company

By the time he conducted America's first transcontinental telephone call in 1915, Alexander Graham Bell's name was well known both in the United States and abroad. He had little to do with the telephone in his later years, but his early success in invention, as well as his imposing presence in the scientific and intellectual communities, made him a celebrity.

FAMILY LIFE

Bell stepped down from the Bell Company board of directors in 1880 and from the company itself a year later. One might think that the telephone's inventor would wish to be along for all that followed, but Bell had a restless, mercurial temperament. He was happy to leave the telephone world at the height of his success and go on to other things.

His marriage to Mabel Hubbard was one of the smartest moves of his life. Alec and May (as they called each other) were truly a devoted couple. At first it may have appeared that he brought more to the marriage because he was a successful man of the world, but over the years she proved to be his equal and more. Where Bell was restless and fidgety, she was calm and determined, and she probably managed their household and financial lives better than he could have done.

If she made one big mistake (and a forgivable one), it was her insistence that they sell their thousands of shares of Bell Company stock too early. In the heady days that followed the out-of-court settlement with Western Union, Bell Company stock more than doubled to approximately $1,000 per share, and May impressed upon Alec the importance of selling the stock immediately. He did not always follow her advice, and they sold their shares slowly over the next decade. As a result, they became millionaires by a narrow margin, which was far more than they had previously hoped; it also meant that the Bell Company (and later subsidiaries) never produced a true heir or heiress. Unlike the Bells, the Rockefellers held on to their Standard Oil holdings, and other Gilded Age families did the same. Oil, coal, and railroads all produced stupendous wealth that lasted for generations, but this was not the case with the telephone or the Bells. Still, neither Alec nor May seemed to regret this state of affairs. They had a large trust fund, administered by Bell's father-in-law, and they were rich enough to afford a fine home in Washington, D.C.

The nation's capital was delighted to have the Bells in residence. Alexander Graham Bell was invited to join as many prestigious clubs as he could handle at one time. The Bells socialized at dinners and cocktail hours with all the best people in Washington, and many people thought Bell would turn out another masterpiece of invention, for he was still relatively young. He certainly intended to.

Mabel and Alexander Graham Bell are shown together, probably in the 1910s. The Bells were married for 45 years, from 1877 to 1922, when A.G. Bell died.

Bell had always detested hot weather (one thinks of that sweltering day in 1875 when he heard the first twang) and, by the mid-1880s, he wanted a different climate. On a vacation with Mabel, their two young daughters, and Mabel's parents, Bell discovered a remote part of Cape Breton Island, at the very top of Nova Scotia. Here, at Baddeck, on the Bras d'Or, a large saltwater lake, he purchased a good deal of land and began to create a large family estate. Called *Beinn Bhreagh*, which means "beautiful mountain," this land became their home for the rest of their lives. The Bells continued to spend the winter months in Washington, D.C., where they received the acclaim of almost everyone they met in society, but they most preferred life on Cape Breton Island. Geologically quite similar to the Scotland of Bell's youth, the land had powerful emotional associations for Bell.

The Bell clan grew rapidly; their two daughters both married ambitious young men with bright futures. Meanwhile, Bell's parents came to live next door to the Bells in Washington, D.C., and to share life on the Cape Breton estate, too. One of the great and wonderful turnarounds in Bell's life was the esteem and affection that his father had for him. When he was young, Bell had suffered from feelings of inadequacy when compared to his father, and when he was a budding inventor, his father's letters had sometimes stung him, as Melville Bell had a caustic wit. The older Bell grew, and the more aged his father became, the more Bell received the praise and love he had previously missed. Melville Bell's second wife (Bell's mother died in 1897) often reported that her husband's day consisted of asking the same questions again and again: "Where is Alec? Is he well? When will he come?"[1] Bell spent many hours reading to his father, who puffed on his pipe and marveled at the success of his only living son.

Then, too, Bell experienced a turnaround with his father-in-law. Gardiner Greene Hubbard had always guarded Bell's financial interests and given him good advice, but the relationship was tarnished in its early years by Hubbard's disdain for his son-in-law's ignorance about financial matters. This situation

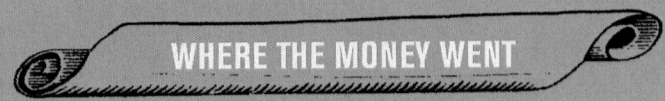

WHERE THE MONEY WENT

When one thinks of oil, the name *Rockefeller* comes to mind. When one thinks of railroads, the family name *Vanderbilt* leaps forward. If someone mentions the personal computer, either Bill Gates or Steve Jobs comes to one's consciousness. The same is true of the telephone, where one immediately thinks of the name *Bell*, but did he become rich?

The Bells were not rich by today's standards. By the time Bell was in his forties, he and his wife probably had a million dollars, perhaps a bit more. They gave generously to some in need, and they were a bit stingy with some other charities. It was a very big deal at the time to have a million dollars; there were probably only about 4,000 millionaires in the entire United States in 1900. Still, it does not remotely compare to today's wealth generated by the computer industry, such as the fortune of Bill Gates, which is approximately $50 or $60 billion.

How successful were the Boston financiers? Most of them— those who came into the business in the 1880s—did well, but did not become fabulously rich. Few became millionaires, but most enjoyed comfortable lives.

As for the new management that came in 1907 under Theodore Vail, few became truly rich. Vail was said to be so absentminded and wasteful that he never saved a dollar when he could spend one. As late as 1976, 100 years after the creation of the telephone, AT&T executives reported salaries in the hundreds of thousands—not millions—of dollars. That changed in the 1980s and 1990s, decades in which CEO (chief executive officer) compensation expanded enormously. Even so, it must be said that most AT&T money was returned either to its shareholders or to the maintenance of its physical plants. The telephone company was a place to make a good living, a secure one, but it was not for those who aspired to great wealth.

was completely reversed in the 1890s, with Hubbard occasionally saying that whatever the matter was, it should be put to Bell, who would have the right answer. Nothing could have been more satisfying to Bell than to have the approbation and admiration of his formerly caustic father and his formerly superior father-in-law.

There were losses as well as gains. Bell's mother died in 1897, and his father died in 1906. His father-in-law died before the turn of the twentieth century, and, quite suddenly, Bell was the true patriarch of the Bell clan. He relished the role, playing with his grandchildren, building enormous toys (some of which had practical applications) and frolicking as he much as he could. Many people commented then, and many biographers have commented since, on how much weight Bell gained soon after his marriage to Mabel Hubbard. It's true that the dark-haired slim man of 29 became overweight and gray in his thirties, but his vigor never departed. To his wife's admonitions that he should eat less, Bell retorted that someone as active as he should not have to worry about calories.

One of his greatest sources of satisfaction came from his sons-in-law, both of whom seemed conscious of the need to do something remarkable to measure up to the Bell name. David Grandison Fairchild, who married Marian Hubbard Bell, was a famous botanist who eventually founded the Fairchild Gardens in Miami, Florida, and Gilbert Grosvenor, married to Elsie May Bell, became the first full-time editor of *National Geographic* magazine. When he asked his august father-in-law about the best way to express the academic aims of the society, Bell replied that it should study "THE WORLD AND ALL THAT IS IN IT."[2] The expression stuck, and remains the motto of today's National Geographic Society.

WORK LIFE

With his large family, one might think that Bell had put inventing aside. Nothing could be further from the truth. He actually doubled his efforts over the years, spending more time alone in his workshop and laboratory than ever before.

Fascinated by the possibilities of flight, Bell spent many hours in consultation with Samuel P. Langley, first secretary of the Smithsonian Institution. Bell and Langley worked hard to create a high-powered engine, one strong enough to launch a craft into the air, but most of their efforts were thwarted by their lack of knowledge. In the end, it was Wilbur and Orville Wright who, unsupported by grants or governments, discovered the mysteries of flight. Their success at Kitty Hawk, North Carolina, in 1903 was followed by a spectacular air demonstration around New York City in 1909, all but sealing their names as the founders of human flight. Bell did not publicly comment on their success, but he may have smiled to himself, knowing that as a young man of 29 he had surpassed the best engineers of Western Union Company. Still, he did not stop.

Bell continued to work right up to the end. He experimented with hydrofoils, with the beginnings of catamaran boats, and he may have been the first person to describe the greenhouse effect, in which high levels of carbon emissions on Earth create warming conditions. Despite his physical bulk, he was as active as ever.

If there was one thing Mabel Bell could not cure in her husband it was his desire to work late into the night and arise late in the morning. This became a habit during his late twenties, and neither his wife nor anyone else could convince him to shake it. Bell often worked until 1:00 or 2:00 A.M., and then slept soundly until 10:00 or 11:00 A.M.; relatives claimed they never knew a man harder to awaken.

All the vigor notwithstanding, Bell did slow down. His father had died from complications from diabetes at the age of 86, and Bell had the same ailment by his seventies. He did his best to control his strong appetite, but grandchildren would often relate how he would sneak a piece of pie (and make sure

Alexander Graham Bell is seen with his granddaughters Gertrude Grosvenor, left, and Mabel Grosvenor, right, as he holds Lilian Waters Grosvenor, at Beinn Bhreagh in Baddeck, Nova Scotia in this 1908 photo.

they got one too). Mabel Hubbard, who remained slim well into her sixties, could only shake her head.

Bell continued to defy nature. "Never felt better in my life," he told a friend as he neared his seventieth birthday,[3] but he was actually beginning to lose strength. The end came on August 2, 1922. Bell died peacefully, at the age of 75, at his beloved estate on Cape Breton Island. Mabel Bell, who was in excellent health at that point, died five months later of pancreatic cancer on January 3, 1923.

The world reacted. There were lengthy obituaries in all of the major newspapers; condolences poured in from as far away as Japan, which the Bells had visited in 1896. One of the most poignant descriptions of all came from Thomas A. Watson. He and his wife were hiking in the Colorado Mountains in the summer of 1922, and on reaching their cabin one evening, Watson found a telegram announcing the death of his colleague. Although Watson and Bell had not been in close touch over the years, they retained a strong fondness for each other, which is apparent from Watson's reaction:

> And with my sorrow for the passing of the man who had meant so much in my life came a sense of loneliness as I realized that I was the last of the little group [Bell, Sanders, Hubbard, and Watson] so closely and happily associated in our telephone struggles and successes nearly half a century before. It cannot be long before I must follow my old associate into the cloud, but I have faith that the sun shines beyond.[4]

AT&T IN 1922

In the year Alexander Graham Bell died, American Telephone and Telegraph had become one of the greatest of all American companies. This does not mean it was the most loved or the most admired; there were plenty of people who criticized AT&T, and even some who truly loathed it. Despite this, the company had become as important as General Electric or as Ford Motor Company; it was one of the titans of American industry. Some of the statistics offered by Moody's Manual (the predecessor of Standard & Poor's) offer testimony. In the year Bell died, AT&T:

> Had 9,514,813 telephones in operation;
> Was connected to another 4,535,752 phones, for a
>   total of 14,050,565;
> Had 8,184,372 miles (13,171,470 kilometers) of wire
>   above ground;
> Had 18,222,913 miles (29,326,936 kilometers) below
>   ground, for a total of 26,407,285 miles (42,498,406
>   kilometers); and
> Had 240,000 stockholders.[5]

These staggering statistics indicate the strength of the Bell companies. It is true that the independent telephone companies were not gone—according to Moody's Manual, there were 10,200 separate ones—but the Bell companies now had more than two-thirds of the total market, and they never looked back.

AT&T never found another overall leader as charismatic or as broad-spirited as Theodore N. Vail. The company's image suffered over the decades that followed, largely because it enjoyed such a monopoly on telephone use. One of the most derogatory studies of the company came out in 1939, when the effects of the Great Depression were still apparent. N.R. Danielian's *AT&T: The Story of Industrial Conquest* made the telephone company appear to be a giant hydra, sucking on the life blood of millions of Americans. Much that Danielian said was true, especially about the ways that AT&T had systematically destroyed its early competition, but one has to ask: Would the nation have been better off without AT&T? Would wholesale competition have been better than a regulated monopoly?

The question was raised again by John Brooks. In 1976, he penned *Telephone: The First Hundred Years* to commemorate a century of the telephone. Granted unlimited access to AT&T's corporate records, Brooks also spent time with the managers of the company in the early 1970s. Here is how he described those he met at 195 Broadway, AT&T's permanent New York City headquarters:

> There is a certain sameness about AT&T people. Their dress and manner is conservative, but not to the point of stuffiness; they keep their neckties on in their offices, but their shirts are not necessarily white nor their ties narrow and subdued. They seem far more vivid, dashing, and enterprising than a handful of government bureaucrats, but far less so than, say, the brainy and hungry young hotshots of some rising new high-technology company. Almost to a man, the top ones, like their boss, John deButts, are lifetime Bell System careerists.[6]

Brooks refrained from answering the great question of whether America would be better off with or without AT&T, but most Americans of that time were against the communications giant. Their hopes came to fruition in January 1984, when AT&T was broken up into eight different, smaller companies as a result of a U.S. government court injunction.

THE TELEPHONE IN 1922

In 1922, the telephone had become a nearly indispensable part of American life. True, millions of American households did not yet have a phone, but most of them wanted to have one. What was a convenience for most urban dwellers had become an absolute necessity for many rural ones. Americans living on the Great Plains or in the Rocky Mountains could bear almost any amount of isolation as long as they could pick up the telephone and hear someone else's voice.

It cannot be disputed that the telephone is an enormous success. One has to ask the difficult question: Does Alexander

Graham Bell deserve the enormous credit he has received for more than a century?

The answer is yes. Working alone for two years, and then with Watson for two more, Bell independently came to the conclusion that the human voice could be transmitted electrically. It is certainly true that the means for doing this had existed for almost 40 years, and that the telephone could have been invented as early as 1845, but no one else put together the different elements of the equation. Blessed with a terrific sense of hearing, as well as a great knowledge of how the voice works, Bell was able to put together the other parts, including batteries, acid, membranes, and the use of electrical current. There is not the slightest doubt that someone else could have done the same thing, or that they would have done it if he had not, but the credit belongs to Bell, who was first on the scene.

CHRONOLOGY

1847 **March 3** Alexander Bell is born in Edinburgh, Scotland.

1858 Alexander Bell takes *Graham* as his middle name.

1863 Bell goes to London to live with his grandfather, Alexander Bell Sr.

1864 Bell teaches at the Elgin School.

1865 Bell's grandfather, Alexander Bell Sr., dies.

1867 Bell's father, Alexander Melville Bell, publishes *Visible Speech: The Science of Universal Alphabetics.*

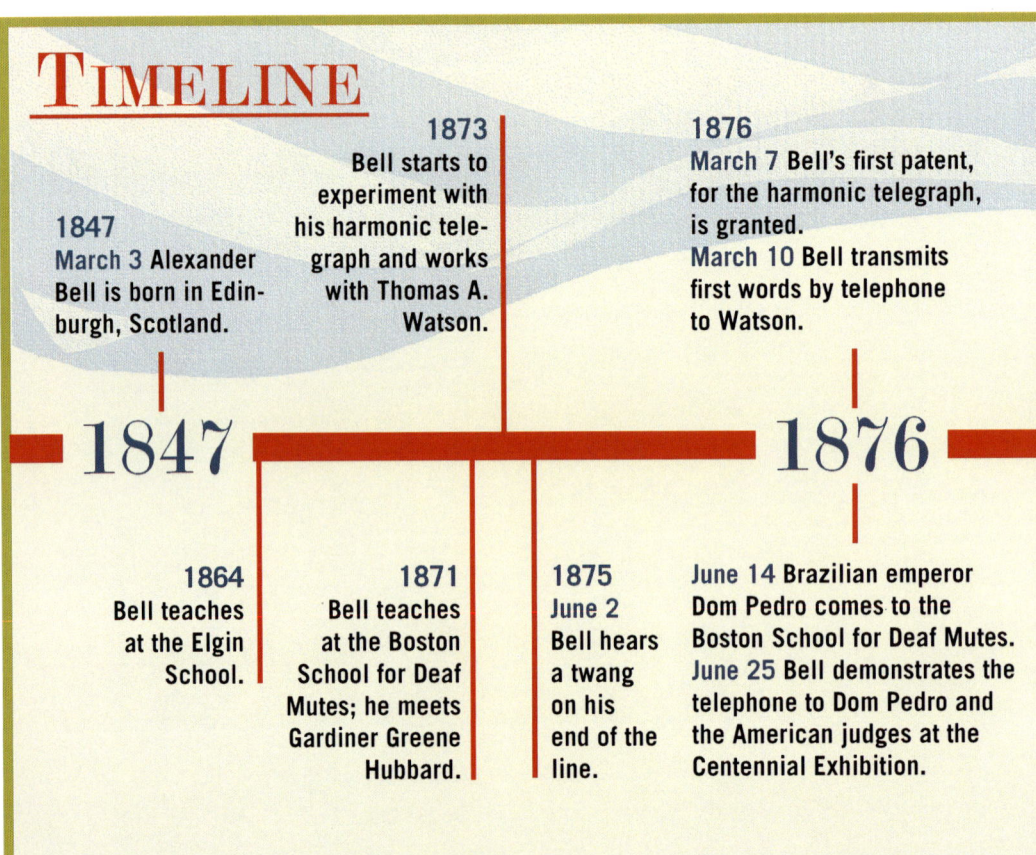

TIMELINE

1873
Bell starts to experiment with his harmonic telegraph and works with Thomas A. Watson.

1876
March 7 Bell's first patent, for the harmonic telegraph, is granted.
March 10 Bell transmits first words by telephone to Watson.

1847
March 3 Alexander Bell is born in Edinburgh, Scotland.

1847   1876

1864
Bell teaches at the Elgin School.

1871
Bell teaches at the Boston School for Deaf Mutes; he meets Gardiner Greene Hubbard.

1875
June 2 Bell hears a twang on his end of the line.

June 14 Brazilian emperor Dom Pedro comes to the Boston School for Deaf Mutes.
June 25 Bell demonstrates the telephone to Dom Pedro and the American judges at the Centennial Exhibition.

1867   Bell's younger brother, Ted Bell, dies of tuberculosis.

1870   Bell's older brother, Melly Bell, dies of the same disease.

1870   The remaining Bells move to Brantford, Ontario.

1871   Bell teaches at the Boston School for Deaf Mutes; he meets Gardiner Greene Hubbard.

1872   Bell starts to teach Georgie Sanders, a five-year-old deaf boy.

1873   Bell begins to experiment with his harmonic telegraph and works with Thomas A. Watson.

1875   **June 2** Bell hears a twang on his end of the line.

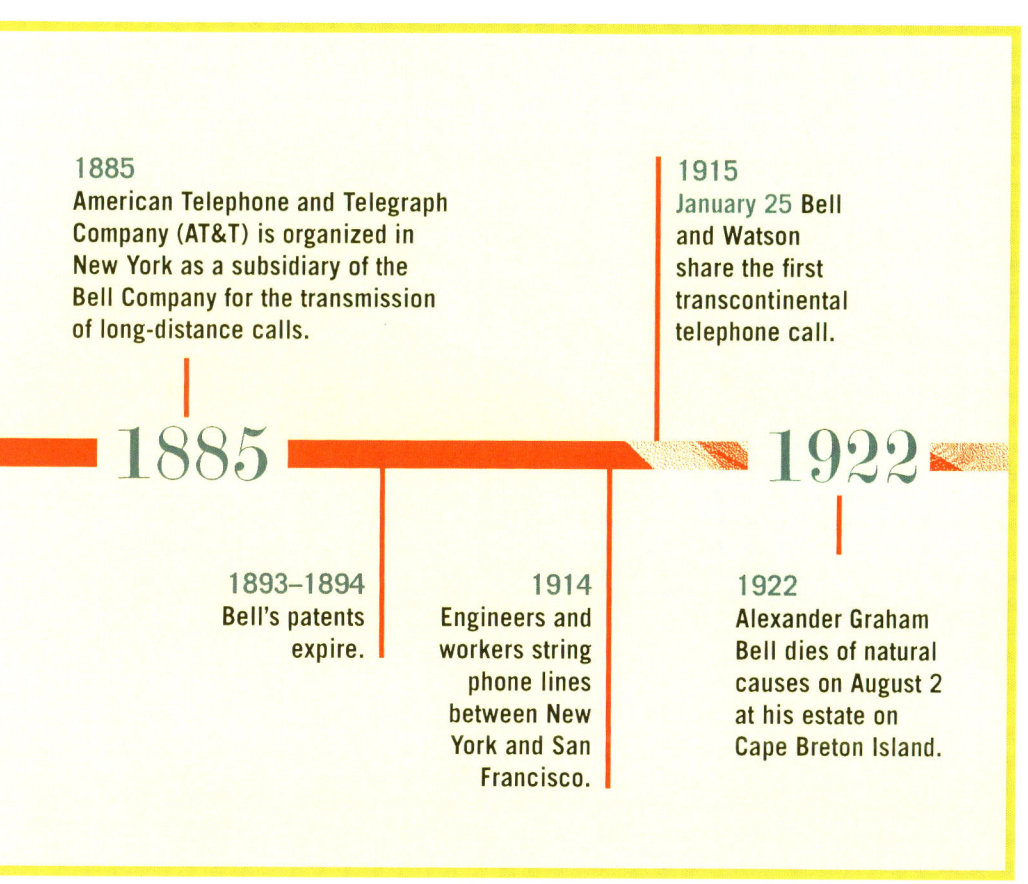

1885
American Telephone and Telegraph Company (AT&T) is organized in New York as a subsidiary of the Bell Company for the transmission of long-distance calls.

1915
January 25 Bell and Watson share the first transcontinental telephone call.

1885   1922

1893–1894
Bell's patents expire.

1914
Engineers and workers string phone lines between New York and San Francisco.

1922
Alexander Graham Bell dies of natural causes on August 2 at his estate on Cape Breton Island.

1876   **March 7** Bell's first patent, for the harmonic telegraph, is granted.

March 10 Bell communicates the immortal first words to be transmitted by telephone to Watson.

June 14 Brazilian emperor Dom Pedro comes to the Boston School for Deaf Mutes.

June 18 Bell leaves for Philadelphia.

June 25 Bell demonstrates the telephone to Dom Pedro and the American judges at the Centennial Exhibition on June 25.

1877   **July 9** Bell's second patent, for the magneto transmitter of the human voice, is granted; Bell, Watson, Hubbard, and Sanders form the first telephone company, the Bell Company.

July 11 Bell marries Mabel Hubbard and they leave for Europe.

1878   **June 14** Bell demonstrates the telephone to Queen Victoria.

1879   **November 10** Bell Company wins an out-of-court settlement against Western Union Telegraph Company in the *Dowd* case, which granted the Bell Company a monopoly for the next 14 years.

1880   The National Bell Telephone Company becomes the American Bell Telephone Company.

1885   American Telephone and Telegraph Company (AT&T) is organized in New York as a wholly owned subsidiary of the Bell Company for the transmission of long-distance calls.

1888   Telephone service is interrupted in New York City as a result of the Blizzard of '88; project is begun to lay underground telephone lines.

1888	Theodore N. Vail resigns as president of AT&T.
1893–1894	Bell's patents expire.
1906	Bell's father, Alexander Melville Bell, dies.
1907	Theodore N. Vail returns as president of AT&T.
1913	Lee De Forest sells his patent for the first triode vacuum tube to AT&T.
1914	Engineers and workers string phone lines between New York and San Francisco.
1915	**January 25** Bell and Watson share the first transcontinental telephone call.
1918	The federal government seizes AT&T during World War I.
1918	AT&T returns to business as usual.
1919	Theodore N. Vail resigns as president of AT&T.
1920	Theodore N. Vail dies.
1922	**August 2** Alexander Graham Bell dies of natural causes at his estate on Cape Breton Island.
1923	**January 23** Mabel Hubbard Bell dies.

NOTES

CHAPTER 1

1. "A.G. Bell to Melville and Eliza Bell, April 16, 1871." Alexander Graham Bell Family Papers at the Library of Congress. http://memory.loc.gov/ammem/bellhtml/bellhome.html.

CHAPTER 2

1. "The Ocean Telegraph," *New York Times.* (17 August 1858): p. 1.
2. Ibid.

CHAPTER 3

1. Robert V. Bruce, *Bell: Alexander Graham Bell and the Conquest of Solitude.* Ithaca, N.Y.: Cornell University Press, 1973, p. 26.
2. Ibid., pp. 33–34.
3. Alexander Melville Bell, *Visible Speech: The Science of Universal Alphabetics.* London: Simpkin, Marshall, 1867, p. 21.

CHAPTER 4

1. Robert V. Bruce, *Bell*, pp. 67–68.
2. Ibid., p. 59.

CHAPTER 5

1. Thomas A. Watson, *The Birth and Babyhood of the Telephone.* New York: Telephone Review, p. 9.
2. Ibid., p. 10.
3. Ibid., p. 12.
4. Robert V. Bruce, *Bell*, p. 100.
5. "A.G. Bell to Melville and Eliza Bell," http://memory.loc.gov/ammem/bellhtml/bellhome.html.

CHAPTER 6

1. "Bell to His Parents," March 18, 1875. http://memory.loc.gov/ammem/bellhtml/bellhome.html.
2. Ibid.
3. Ibid.
4. Thomas A. Watson, *Exploring Life.* New York: D. Appleton, 1926, pp. 66–67.
5. Ibid., p. 67.
6. Lewis Coe, *The Telephone and Its Several Inventors.* Jefferson, N.C. McFarland, 1995, p. 214.
7. Edwin S. Grosvenor and Morgan Wesson, *Alexander Graham Bell: The Life and Times of the Man Who Invented the Telephone.* New York: Harry N. Abrams, 1997, p. 67.

CHAPTER 7

1. "Bell to Mabel Hubbard," June 18, 1876. http://memory.loc.gov/ammem/bellhtml/bellhome.html.
2. Robert V. Bruce, *Bell*, p. 197.
3. Ibid.
4. "The Speaking Telegraph," *New York Times.* May 20, 1877, p. 2
5. Ibid.

CHAPTER 8

1. Thomas A. Watson, *Exploring Life*, p. 170.

CHAPTER 9

1. Lewis Coe, *The Telephone and Its Several Inventors*, p. 8.
2. Rocky Collins and Matthew Collins (III), directors, *The Telephone*, VHS, PBS Video, 1997.
3. Emily Post, *Etiquette in Society, in Business, in Politics and at Home.* New York: Funk & Wagnalls, 1922, p. 128.
4. Ibid.
5. *Views on Public Questions: A Collection of Papers and Addresses of Theodore Newton Vail, 1907–1917.* Private printing, 1917, p 11.
6. "Phone to Pacific from the Atlantic," *New York Times.* (26 January 1915): p. 2.
7. Ibid.
8. *Views on Public Questions,* p. 369.

CHAPTER 10

1. Robert V. Bruce, *Bell,* p. 422.
2. Ibid., p. 425.
3. Ibid., p. 486.
4. Thomas A.Watson, *Exploring Life,* pp. 314–315.
5. *Moody's Manual of Railroads and Corporation Securities: Public Utility Section, 1923.* New York: Poor's Publishing, 1923, pp. 1360–1361.
6. John Brooks, *Telephone: The First Hundred Years.* New York: Harper & Row, 1975, p. 27.

BIBLIOGRAPHY

Bell, Alexander Melville. *Visible Speech: The Science of Universal Alphabetics.* London: Simpkin, Marshall, 1867.

Bodnais, David. *Electric Universe: How Electricity Switched on the Modern World.* New York: Three Rivers, 2005.

Brooks, John. *Telephone: The First Hundred Years.* New York: Harper & Row, 1975.

Bruce, Robert V. *Bell: Alexander Graham Bell and the Conquest of Solitude.* Ithaca, N.Y.: Cornell University Press, 1973.

Coe, Lewis. *The Telephone and Its Several Inventors.* Jefferson, N.C.: McFarland, 1995.

Collins, Rocky and Matthew (III). *The Telephone.* VHS. PBS Home Video, 1997.

Danielian, N.R. *AT&T: The Story of Industrial Conquest.* New York: Vanguard Press, 1939.

Finn, Bernard S. "Alexander Graham Bell's Experiments with the Variable-Resistance Transmitter." *Smithsonian Journal of History* 1, no. 4 (1967).

Grosvenor, Edwin S., and Morgan Wesson. *Alexander Graham Bell: The Life and Times of the Man Who Invented the Telephone.* New York: Harry N. Abrams, 1997.

Paine, Albert Bigelow. *In One Man's Life: Being Chapters from the Personal and Business Career of Theodore N. Vail.* New York: Harper, 1921.

Poor's Publishing Company, ed. *Moody's Manual of Railroads and Corporation Securities: Public Utility Section, 1923.* New York: Poor's, 1923.

Post, Emily. *Etiquette in Society, in Business, in Politics and at Home.* New York: Funk & Wagnalls, 1922.

Rhodes, Frederick Leland. *Beginnings of Telephony.* New York: Harper, 1929.

Watson, Thomas A. *The Birth and Babyhood of the Telephone.* New York: Telephone Review, 1913.

———. *Exploring Life.* New York: D. Appleton, 1926.

Further Reading

Bodnais, David. *Electric Universe: How Electricity Switched on the Modern World*. New York: Three Rivers, 2005.

Bruce, Robert V. *Bell: Alexander Graham Bell and the Conquest of Solitude*. Ithaca, N.Y.: Cornell University Press, 1973.

Grosvenor, Edwin S., and Morgan Wesson. *Alexander Graham Bell: The Life and Times of the Man Who Invented the Telephone*. New York: Harry N. Abrams, 1997.

Parker, Barry. *Science 101: Physics*. New York: HarperCollins, 2007.

Strandage, Tom. *The Victorian Internet: The Remarkable Story of the Telegraph and the Nineteenth Century's Online Pioneers*. New York: Berkeley Books, 1998.

Waite, Helen Elmira. *Make a Joyful Sound: The Romance of Mabel Hubbard and Alexander Graham Bell*. Philadelphia: Macrae Smith, 1961.

WEB SITES

The Alexander Graham Bell Family Papers at the Library of Congress. Available online. URL: http://memory.loc.gov/ammem/bellhtml/bellhome.html.

Photo Credits

INDEX

ABOUT THE AUTHOR

SAMUEL WILLARD CROMPTON lives and works in the Berkshire Hills of his native western Massachusetts. A part-time professor at Westfield State College and Holyoke Community College, he is also a full-time writer, with books published on topics as diverse as lighthouses, spiritual leaders, and travel narratives. Crompton has always been a lover of the telephone, but he much prefers conversations based on land lines to those carried by satellites.